S0-ACZ-468

GROWTH IN
SPELLING

William N. Novicky

Sophie Dorocak

Marie Colette Faulhaber

Mary Himes

Kathleen McNerney

Rita Petruziello

Ruth Wolfert

SECOND EDITION

LAIDLAW BROTHERS • PUBLISHERS
A Division of Doubleday & Company, Inc.

RIVER FOREST, ILLINOIS
Irvine, California   Chamblee, Georgia   Dallas, Texas   Toronto, Canada

ISBN 0-8445-2327-5

Copyright © 1979   by Laidlaw Brothers, Publishers
A Division of Doubleday & Company, Inc.

All rights reserved. No part of this publication may be reproduced or trans-
mitted in any form or by any means, electronic or mechanical, including
photocopy, recording, or any information storage or retrieval system, without
permission in writing from the publisher.

Printed in the United States of America

89 10 11 12 13 14 15   7654

Contents

Handwriting Chart

Aa Bb Cc Dd

Ee Ff Gg Hh

Ii Jj Kk Ll

Mm Nn Oo Pp

Qq Rr Ss Tt

Uu Vv Ww Xx

Yy Zz

Handwriting by P. Z. Bloser. Used with the permission of ZANER-BLOSER, Inc., publisher of handwriting texts and materials.

Learning to Spell a New Word

Look

Look at the word you want to learn to spell. Say it aloud.

Listen

Close your eyes. Say the word again, and listen to its sounds.

Spell

Look at the word again. Note the letter or letters that spell each sound.

Write

Look at the word and write it. Say the word as you write it.

Think

Close your eyes. Think about how the word is spelled. Move your lips as you spell the word silently.

Write

Write the word again. Check your spelling with the word in the book.

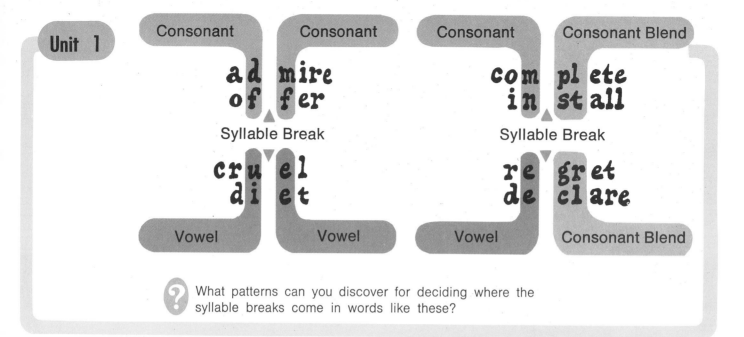

Consonant | **Consonant** | **Consonant** | **Consonant Blend**

ad mire
of fer
Syllable Break

com pl ete
in st all
Syllable Break

cru el
di et

re gr et
de cl are

Vowel | **Vowel** | **Vowel** | **Consonant Blend**

What patterns can you discover for deciding where the syllable breaks come in words like these?

 A   **Syllable Patterns**

Say the list words at the right. Decide how many syllables they have. Then decide where the syllable break comes in each word.

1. Write the list words in which the syllable break comes between two consonants.

2. Write the list words in which the syllable break comes between two vowels.

3. Write the list words in which the syllable break comes between a consonant and a consonant blend.

4. Write the list words in which the syllable break comes between a vowel and a consonant blend.

absorb
accent
adverb
assist
betray
complaint
conflict
dial
effect
expert

extreme
fluid
impart
income
neutral
oblong
pliers
reclaim
restrict
victim

B Check the Spelling

1. Write the list words represented by the dictionary re-spellings below. Check with the dictionary pronunciation key on page 115 if you need help with any of the symbols.

a. /ob' lông/

b. /nü' trəl/

c. /ak' sent/

d. /dī' əl/

e. /flü' id/

f. /kəm plānt'/

g. /vik' təm/

h. /in' kum'/

i. /ad' verb'/

j. /bi trā'/

k. /kon' flikt/

l. /ə sist'/

2. Write the list words that begin with the prefix **re−**.

3. Write the list words that begin with the prefix **ex−**.

Check the Meaning

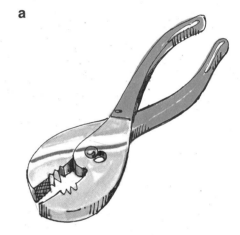

a

1. Write the list words that name the objects in pictures **a** and **b.**

2. Write the list words that go with the definitions below. Check with the Speller Dictionary if you need help with any meanings.

b

a. a fight or struggle

b. to make known

c. longer than wide

d. to help

e. excessive

f. a liquid

g. to soak up

h. a result

i. a tool for grasping

j. to be unfaithful to

Can You Spell   can't   doesn't   won't

C Take the First Spelling Test

7

D Word Challenge

Study the patterns in the chart below. They show how to form and write contractions.

Contractions with **not**	Other Contractions
do not → don't was not → wasn't	that is → that's they are → they're

Now see if you can follow the same patterns as you write contractions for these pairs of words.

1. are not 3. have not 5. there is 7. he has
2. were not 4. could not 6. you are 8. they will

Word Lore

Americans have taken a number of American Indian words into our language, although they have usually changed the pronunciation in the process. **Squash** and **hominy,** for example, are both of American Indian origin. The original Indian words were **askutasquash** and **rockahominy.**

1. Each picture at the right is labeled with its original Indian name. Write the words as we spell them today.

2. Below are the original forms of two more Indian words that Americans have taken into our language. See if you can show how we spell these words today.

a. makasin b. papeisses

a. apasum

b. arahkun

c. moos

Can You Spell

| aren't | moccasin | raccoon | weren't |
| chipmunk | opossum | they're | you're |

d. atchitamon

E Take the Second Spelling Test

8

ná∙vy
Syllable Break

1 The first syllable is stressed and the vowel is long.

gran∙ite
Syllable Break

2 The first syllable is stressed and the vowel is not long.

re∙port′
Syllable Break

3 The first syllable is not stressed.

 What three patterns can you discover for dividing words that have just one consonant at the syllable break?

 A **More Syllable Patterns**

Say the list words at the right. Decide how many syllables each word has. Then decide where the syllable breaks come in the words.

1. Write the list words that have two syllables. Draw lines showing where the syllable breaks come in the words.

2. Write the list words that have three syllables. Draw lines showing where the syllable breaks come.

3. Write the list words that have four syllables. Draw lines showing where the syllable breaks come.

adapt
basis
bonus
decade
deny
dignity
diploma
domestic
identity
majority

museum
pleasant
poverty
premium
recreation
society
syrup
tropical
typical
vitamin

Check the Spelling

1. Write the list word represented by each dictionary respelling below. Then underline the letters that spell the unstressed vowel sound represented by /ə/. Check with the pronunciation key on page 115 and the word list at the right if you need help.

a. /bō′ nəs/

b. /dig′ nə tē/

c. /myü zē′ əm/

d. /də mes′ tik/

e. /rek′ rē ā′ shən/

f. /vī′ tə min/

2. Write the list words in which the vowel sound in the first syllable is spelled with **y.**

Check the Meaning

Write the list words that you could use to replace the words in heavy type. Check with the Speller Dictionary if you need help with any meanings.

1. The nation had a **ten-year period** of prosperity.

2. I enjoy living in a democratic **community.**

3. Was it difficult for you to **adjust** to a new job?

4. The lawyers found a **common ground** for agreement.

5. I saved enough wrappers to receive a **prize.**

6. Did you have **fair** weather for your picnic?

7. Tasha lives in a **hot and humid** climate.

8. Did the principal **refuse** our request?

9. The police learned the **name** of the thief.

10. Our goal is to lessen **want** in this city.

adapt
basis
bonus
decade
deny
dignity
diploma
domestic
identity
majority
museum
pleasant
poverty
premium
recreation
society
syrup
tropical
typical
vitamin

Can You Spell   easy   many   vacation

C   **Take the First Spelling Test**

D Word Challenge

Study the patterns in the chart below for forming plural nouns.

When **y** Follows a Consonant	grocery → groceries liberty → liberties
When **y** Follows a Vowel	monkey → monkeys alley → alleys

Now see if you can apply the same patterns in writing the plurals of these nouns.

1. ability
2. essay
3. variety
4. journey
5. tourney
6. survey
7. balcony
8. diary

Word Lore

Some American Indian words now a part of our language came into English about 400 years ago by way of Spanish. The word **hurricane** is a typical example. The pronunciation of the original Indian word **hurakan** was changed by the Spanish and spelled **huracan.** The English later changed this pronunciation and spelled the new word **hurricane.**

1. Each picture at the right is labeled with its original Indian name. Write the words as we spell them today.

2. Below are the original forms of two more Indian words that have come into our language by way of Spanish. See if you can show how we spell these words today.

    a. tomatl   b. tabaco

Can You Spell

abilities	barbecue	diaries	surveys
balconies	chocolate	hammock	tobacco

E Take the Second Spelling Test

a. American Indian   canoa

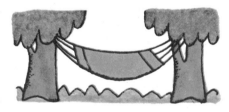

b. American Indian   hamaca

c. American Indian   barbacoa

d. American Indian   chocolatl

Which frog do you think would have better luck in learning to spell this long word? Why?

A Spelling by Syllables

Say the list words at the right. Decide how many syllables each word contains. Then practice spelling the words aloud, syllable by syllable.

1. Write the list words that have four syllables. Remember to think of the words syllable by syllable as you write.

2. Write the list words that have five syllables. Remember to think of the words syllable by syllable as you write.

application
certificate
combination
compensation
computation
conservation
continuation
electricity
expectation
expedition

explanation
interjection
invitation
irrigation
negotiations
reputation
reservation
satisfactory
simplicity
transcontinental

12

Check the Spelling

a

1. Write the list words that have a double consonant.

2. Write the list words that begin with the following prefixes.

    a. **con–**   b. **com–**   c. **re–**   d. **ex–**

Check the Meaning

b

1. Each picture at the right is a clue to a list word. Which word goes with picture **a**? With picture **b**? With picture **c**? Write the words.

2. Copy the following sentences. Complete each one with a list word. Check with the Speller Dictionary if you need help with any meanings.

    a. The owner of this store has a – for honesty.

    b. The patient was in – condition.

    c. Do you have my hotel –?

    d. The clerk made a mistake in his –.

    e. Do you have a birth –?

    f. I slipped and fell in the – ditch.

    g. I received an – to a birthday party.

    h. Janice filled out an – for the job.

    i. Smog is a – of smoke and fog.

    j. Which explorer led the – to the North Pole?

c

Can You Spell   surely   truly   wrote

C   **Take the First Spelling Test**

D Word Challenge

Study the chart at the right to discover two patterns for forming the plurals of nouns that end with **f** or **fe.** Then see if you can apply the patterns in writing the plurals of these words.

1. proof   3. half   5. gulf
2. knife   4. leaf   6. wolf

Word Lore

A full half of the states in the United States have names of American Indian origin. **Nebraska,** for example, comes from **ne-brath-ka,** an Indian word that means "flat water." **Kentucky** comes from **ken-tah-ten,** an Indian word that means "a prairie."

Use the following clues to discover ten more states that have names of American Indian origin. Write the state names.

1. **alakshak,** great peninsula
2. **massa-adchu-es-et,** people living near the big hills
3. **ute,** people living in the mountains
4. **alibamu,** people who make clearings
5. **arizonac,** little springs
6. **arkansaw,** people going with the current
7. **quinnitukq-ut,** near the long river
8. **iliniwek,** men
9. **emissourita,** people living on the big muddy river
10. **wishkonsing,** region of beaver holes

Plurals of Nouns Ending
with f or fe

1. Most nouns just add **−s.**
   belief → beliefs
   giraffe → giraffes

2. The following nouns are exceptions. They change the **f** or **fe** to **v** and add **−es.**

calf	loaf
elf	self
half	shelf
knife	thief
leaf	wife
life	wolf

Can You Spell

beliefs	gulfs	knives	proofs
giraffes	halves	leaves	wolves

E Take the Second Spelling Test

14

Unit 4

The window's fixed, so now I'll have to give it an /as′ pər ən/.

An /as′ prən/! Why?

Because now it has a /pān/.

Which person do you think would be more likely to spell the word **aspirin** correctly? Why?

A Disappearing Syllables

1. Listen as your teacher says the list words. Decide how many syllables each word has. Then decide whether any of the syllables "disappear" when you say the words in ordinary conversation. If they do, you will have to be particularly careful with the words when you come to spell them. Remember that it is all right to lose a syllable in words like these when you talk, but it is never all right to lose a syllable when you write.

2. Write the list words on your own paper. Look up the words in the Speller Dictionary, and draw lines to show where the syllable breaks come in each word. Then practice pronouncing each word. Make sure you sound all the syllables.

accidentally
aspirin
bachelor
cabinet
continually
corporal
criminal
dangerous
decimal
desperate

eventually
experiment
favorite
liberal
marvelous
miniature
prosperous
revenue
theory
treasury

15

Check the Spelling

1. Write the list word represented by each dictionary respelling below. Then underline the letters that spell the unstressed vowel sound represented by /ə/. Check with the pronunciation key on page 115 if you need help.

    a. /kab′ ə nit/   d. /krim′ ə nəl/

    b. /thē′ ər ē/   e. /ek sper′ ə mənt/

    c. /bach′ ə lər/   f. /min′ ē ə chu̇r/

2. Write the list words that end with the suffix —ous.

Check the Meaning

Write the list words that you could use to replace the words in heavy type. Check with the Speller Dictionary if you need help with any meanings.

1. Slow down at that **hazardous** intersection.

2. Our efforts will succeed **in time.**

3. The customer bought a bottle of **pain reliever.**

4. We saw a **very small** dollhouse in that store.

5. Did Greta fall **by chance?**

6. That mechanic has a **successful** business.

7. We found ourselves in a **hopeless** situation.

8. My cousin talks **without stopping.**

9. Thank you for your **generous** donation.

10. The state gets **income** from taxes.

Can You Spell   now   ready   women

Take the First Spelling Test

accidentally
aspirin
bachelor
cabinet
continually
corporal
criminal
dangerous
decimal
desperate
eventually
experiment
favorite
liberal
marvelous
miniature
prosperous
revenue
theory
treasury

D   Word Challenge

Study the chart at the right to discover two patterns for forming the plurals of nouns that end with **o.** Then see if you can apply the patterns in writing the plurals of these words.

1. studio
2. veto
3. soprano
4. echo
5. hero
6. torpedo
7. potato
8. cameo
9. tomato

Word Lore

Use the following clues to discover ten more states that have names of American Indian origin. Write the state names.

1. **ida ho,** salmon tribe
2. **ayuhwa,** sleepy people
3. **kansa,** wind people
4. **minisota,** clear water
5. **mishigamaw,** great lake
6. **misi sipi,** big river
7. **oheo,** beautiful
8. **okla humma,** red people
9. **tanasi,** friends
10. **tejas,** friends

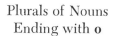

Plurals of Nouns
Ending with **o**

1. Most nouns just add **–s.**

banjo → banjos
kangaroo → kangaroos

2. The following nouns are exceptions because they always add **–es.**

echo	tomato
hero	torpedo
potato	veto

Can You Spell

banjos	heroes	sopranos	torpedoes
echoes	kangaroos	studios	vetoes

E   Take the Second Spelling Test

A Single and Double Consonants

In spelling a word like **piccalilli,** you may have found it hard sometimes to remember which consonant sounds are spelled with single letters and which are spelled with double letters. The list words at the right present the same kind of spelling problem. Some of the words contain just single consonants, while others contain both single and double consonants. The most efficient way to learn to spell these words is to use the study helps on page 5.

1. Write the list words that contain just single consonants.

2. Write the list words that contain a double consonant.

accomplish
accurate
aluminum
apparent
approach
classify
colonist
colossal
commerce
harass

irrigate
macaroni
nobility
occasion
peninsula
piccolo
sheriff
surrender
tolerate
vanilla

a

1. Write the list word represented by each dictionary respelling below. Then underline the letters that spell the unstressed vowel sound represented by /ə/.

a. /ir′ ə gāt/

d. /kol′ ə nist/

b. /tol′ ə rāt′/

e. /sə ren′ dər/

c. /nō bil′ ə tē/

f. /ə lü′ mə nəm/

2. Write the list word that is related to each of the following words.

a. peninsular

d. approachable

b. classification

e. commercial

c. accuracy

f. apparently

b

Check the Meaning

1. Each picture at the right is a clue to a list word. Which word goes with picture **a?** With picture **b?** With picture **c?** Write the words.

c

Words that have the same or nearly the same meaning are called **synonyms. Brave** and **bold** are **synonyms,** and so are **unhappy** and **sad.**

2. Write the list words that go with the following pairs of synonyms.

a. perform, complete

e. obvious, evident

b. gigantic, enormous

f. annoy, vex

c. trade, business

g. event, happening

d. allow, endure

h. precise, exact

Can You Spell   again   any   busy

C Take the First Spelling Test

Word Challenge

Singular Nouns	the **speaker's** notes my **friend's** home
Plural Nouns with **−s**	the **campers'** tents the **judges'** seats
Plural Nouns Without **−s**	the **children's** toys the **salesmen's** cars

Study the chart above, which shows how to write the possessive forms of singular and plural nouns. Then write the possessive form of each noun in parentheses.

1. the (lieutenant) order
2. the (candidates) names
3. The (Women) Club
4. the (lawyers) speeches
5. the (surveyor) transit
6. the (policemen) uniforms
7. my (daughters) bicycles
8. (James) coat

Word Lore

Some words that are now a part of our language came into English by way of French-speaking Canadians. **Prairie, lacrosse, caribou, bureau,** and **toboggan** are examples.

Each picture at the right is labeled with its original French name. See if you can write the words as we spell them today.

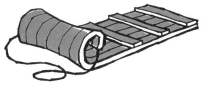

1. French   tobagan

2. French   gaufre

Can You Spell

candidate	daughter	lieutenant	surveyor
caribou	gopher	prairie	toboggan

3. French   chaudiere

E   **Take the Second Spelling Test**

Unit 6 Review and Evaluation

A Review the List Words

Spelling Tip	Always practice spelling a long word like **negotiations** syllable by syllable.

1. Write the list words represented by the dictionary respellings below. Remember to think of the words syllable by syllable as you write. Check with the words at the right if you need help with any spellings.

a. /in′ və tā′ shən/

b. /rep′ yə tā′ shən/

c. /sim plis′ ə tē/

d. /sər tif′ ə kit/

e. /i lek tris′ ə tē/

f. /kon′ sər vā′ shən/

g. /sat′ is fak′ tər ē/

h. /ek′ splə nā′ shən/

Spelling Tip	Take care that you include all the syllables when you write a word like **aspirin,** especially if you do not ordinarily pronounce all the syllables when you speak.

2. Write the list words represented by the dictionary respellings below.

a. /rev′ ə nü/

b. /mär′ və ləs/

c. /fā′ vər it/

d. /kab′ ə nit/

e. /krim′ ə nəl/

f. /pros′ pər əs/

g. /lib′ ər əl/

h. /des′ ə məl/

Spelling Tip	Try using the study helps on page 5 if you have trouble remembering where the double consonant occurs in a word like **piccolo.**

3. The list at the right contains ten words that have one or more double consonants. Find the words, and write them on your paper.

accomplish
apparent
approach
cabinet
certificate
classify
colossal
conservation
criminal
decimal
electricity
explanation
favorite
harass
invitation
irrigation
liberal
marvelous
occasion
prosperous
reputation
revenue
satisfactory
sheriff
simplicity
surrender

More List Words to Review

1. Write the list words represented by the respellings below. Underline the letters that spell an unstressed vowel sound represented by /ə/. Check with the words at the right if you need any help with the spelling.

a. /vī′ tə min/

b. /ak′ sə den′ təl ē/

c. /des′ pər it/

d. /kən tin′ yü ə lē/

e. /ə lü′ mə nəm/

f. /dig′ nə tē/

g. /sə sī′ ə tē/

h. /kôr′ pər əl/

i. /də mes′ tik/

j. /ī den′ tə tē/

accidentally
aluminum
continually
corporal
desperate
dignity
domestic
eventually
expedition
experiment
identity
miniature
museum
neutral
premium
society
syrup
treasury
tropical
typical
vitamin

2. Write **syrup** and **typical.** Underline the letter that spells the vowel sound in the first syllable of each word.

3. Write **neutral** and **treasury.** Underline the letters that spell the vowel sound in the first syllable of each word.

4. Write **experiment** and **expedition.** Underline the letter that spells /ks/ in each word.

5. Write **eventually** and **miniature.** Underline the letter that spells /ch/ in each word.

6. Write **premium** and **museum.** Underline the letter that spells the /ē/ sound in the second syllable of each word.

Take the First Review Test

D   **Review the Challenging Words**

1. Write the plural form of each of the following nouns. Check with the patterns at the right if you need help.

a. knife	g. soprano	m. proof
b. veto	h. leaf	n. kangaroo
c. half	i. diary	o. echo
d. ability	j. giraffe	p. balcony
e. survey	k. banjo	q. wolf
f. studio	l. belief	r. hero

2. Write the following sentences. Complete each sentence with the possessive form of the noun in parentheses.

a. Have you seen (James) puppy?

b. I picked up the (children) toys.

c. The (lawyers) offices are on the same floor.

d. My (friend) bicycle was stolen yesterday.

e. Did you write down the (women) names?

f. Did you hear the (candidates) speeches?

g. What was the (lieutenant) assignment?

h. The (policemen) cars are blue and white.

Can You Spell These Science Words

carbohydrate	germination	oxidation
circulation	gravitation	petroleum
distillation	hibernation	photosynthesis
evaporation	metallurgical	pollination
fertilization	metamorphosis	precipitation

Forming Plurals

Nouns Ending with y

1. Add **−s** when **y** follows a vowel.

monkey → monkeys

2. Change **y** to **i** and add **−es** when **y** follows a consonant.

grocery → groceries

Nouns Ending with o

1. Most nouns just add **−s.**

radio → radios

2. The following exceptions need **−es.**

echo	tomato
hero	torpedo
potato	veto

Nouns Ending with f, fe

1. Most nouns just add **−s.**

roof → roofs

2. The following exceptions change **f** to **v** and add **−es.**

calf	leaf	shelf
elf	life	thief
half	loaf	wife
knife	self	wolf

 E   **Take the Second Review Test**

All right, Champ. Spell /mem' ər ē/.

? I? ? MEM_RY O? A? E? U? ?

His memory has failed.

 Is it surprising that even an elephant could forget the middle vowel spelling in **memory?** Why not?

A The Unstressed Vowel Problem

1. Write each list word below. Supply the letter that spells the unstressed middle vowel sound.

a. rem — dy
b. par — chute
c. dem — nstrate
d. im — tate
e. diff — cult
f. abs — lute
g. court — sy
h. crit — cize
i. di — gram
j. rec — gnize
k. instr — ment
l. circ — mstance

2. Write each list word below. Supply the letter that spells the unstressed final vowel sound.

a. innoc — nt
b. privil — ge
c. skelet — n
d. contin — nt
e. fortun — te
f. delic — te
g. specim — n
h. docum — nt

absolute
circumstance
continent
courtesy
criticize
delicate
demonstrate
diagram
difficult
document

fortunate
imitate
innocent
instrument
parachute
privilege
recognize
remedy
skeleton
specimen

Check the Spelling

1. Write the list words represented by the dictionary re-spellings below. Then underline the letters that spell the vowel sound represented by /ə/ in the unstressed syllables. Check with the pronunciation key on page 115 if you need help with any of the symbols.

a

a. /sėr′ kəm stans/   d. /del′ ə kit/

b. /fôr′ chə nit/   e. /ab′ sə lüt/

c. /kon′ tə nənt/   f. /dok′ yə mənt/

2. Write the list words that begin with the prefix **re–**.

Check the Meaning

b

1. Each picture at the right is a clue to one of the list words. Which list word goes with picture **a**? With picture **b**? With picture **c**? Write the words.

2. Write the list words that you could use to replace the words in heavy type below. Use the Speller Dictionary if you need help with any meanings.

a. Can you **explain** how to operate this machine?

b. What **treatment** did the doctor recommend?

c. This jigsaw puzzle is **hard to do.**

d. We had the **special favor** of meeting the pilot.

e. Laura didn't seem to **notice** us.

f. The accused man was **blameless.**

g. I was amazed by George's **polite behavior.**

c

Can You Spell   Wednesday   Thursday   Saturday

C

Take the First Spelling Test

Word Challenge

Words that name the months of the year often contain unstressed syllables that can cause a spelling problem. Write the month of the year represented by each dictionary respelling below. Then underline all the letters that spell the vowel sound represented by /ə/.

1. /ok tō′ bər/
2. /ā′ prəl/
3. /jù lī′/
4. /di sem′ bər/
5. /jün/
6. /märch/

7. /mā/
8. /ô′ gəst/
9. /jan′ yü er′ ē/
10. /nō vem′ bər/
11. /feb′ rü er′ ē/
12. /sep tem′ bər/

January
February
March
April
May
June
July
August
September
October
November
December

Word Lore

At one time New York was a Dutch colony, and most of the people living there spoke Dutch. One of the results of this is that a number of useful Dutch words came into our language between 1600 and 1800. Examples include **cookie, boss, spook,** and **sleigh.**

1. Each picture at the right is labeled with its original Dutch name. Write the words as we spell them today.

2. The following words are written with their original Dutch spellings. See if you can write each word as we spell it today.

a. daler
b. wagen

c. koolsla
d. docke

a. Dutch   wafel

b. Dutch   cabuse

Can You Spell

| caboose | January | September | sleigh |
| coleslaw | February | October | waffle |

Take the Second Spelling Test

I know comedian has an e, so comedy must have an e, too.

What comes after the m in /kom′ ə dē/, an e or an a?

LAUGHS ❀
❀ UNLIMITED
AN-*Original*
COM

How does the word **comedian** reveal the spelling of the un-stressed middle vowel sound in **comedy?**

A The Comedy–Comedian Pattern

1. The list at the right contains ten pairs of related words. The first word in each pair has an unstressed vowel sound that becomes easier to spell when you think of the second word. Pronounce the list words in pairs to see how this process works.

2. Write the related word that reveals the spelling of an unstressed vowel sound in each word below.

a. definite	f. origin
b. relative	g. human
c. magnet	h. colony
d. admirable	i. horizon
e. victory	j. melody

admirable
admire
colony
colonial
definite
define
horizon
horizontal
human
humanity

magnet
magnetic
melody
melodious
origin
original
relative
relate
victory
victorious

Check the Spelling

1. Write the list words represented by each pair of re-spellings below. Check with the dictionary key on page 115 if you need help with any of the symbols.

a. /hyü′ mən/
/hyü man′ ə tē/

b. /kol′ ə nē/
/kə lō′ nē əl/

c. /ôr′ ə jin/
/ə rij′ ə nəl/

d. /ad′ mər ə bəl/
/ad mīr′/

e. /def′ ə nit/
/di fīn′/

f. /rel′ ə tiv/
/ri lāt′/

2. Write the list words that end with the following suffixes.

a. **−able**   b. **−al**   c. **−ity**   d. **−ous**

3. Write **melodious** and **victorious.** Underline the letter that spells /ē/ in each word.

Check the Meaning

Most pairs of list words have related meanings as well as related forms. Copy the following sentences. Complete each sentence with a pair of list words.

1. All — beings are a part of —.
2. This — has a strong — field.
3. The — team shared their — with the fans.
4. The — notes sounded a familiar —.

admirable
admire

colony
colonial

definite
define

horizon
horizontal

human
humanity

magnet
magnetic

melody
melodious

origin
original

relative
relate

victory
victorious

Can You Spell   straight   too   write

Take the First Spelling Test

Word Challenge

1. Write each of the following words on your paper. Then see if you can write a related word that will reveal the spelling of the unstressed vowel sound in each word.

a. at<u>o</u>m

b. opp<u>o</u>site

c. an<u>a</u>lyze

d. econ<u>o</u>my

e. exp<u>i</u>ration

f. spec<u>i</u>fy

g. nec<u>e</u>ssary

h. pol<u>i</u>cy

2. See if you can complete each sentence below with a pair of related words from exercise 1. Write each complete sentence on your paper.

a. The large — size is the most — buy.

b. The — date shows when the license will —.

Word Lore

The Dutch contributed a small number of place names to our country, most of them in and around New York City. For example, the name **Harlem** comes from the original Dutch name **Haarlem.**

1. The following place names are given in their original Dutch forms. Using a map of New York City, see if you can write each name as we spell it today.

a. Breuckelin   b. Staaten Eylandt

2. All the place names in New York State containing **kill, hook,** and **clove** are also of Dutch origin. Using a map of eastern New York State, make a list of place names containing **kill, hook,** and **clove.**

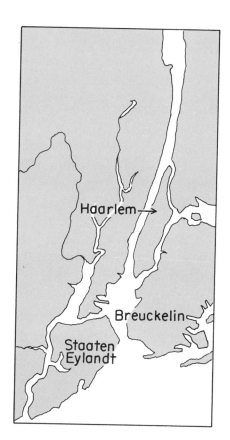

Can You Spell

analysis	economical	necessity	political
atomic	expire	oppose	specific

Take the Second Spelling Test

Group 1

ran' dom

prob' lem

vic' tim

Group 2

com' mon

sev' en

ba' sin

Group 3

pi' lot

car' pet

rab' bit

 Which syllable in each word is easier to spell, the stressed syllable or the unstressed syllable? Why?

A Unstressed Final Syllables

Each list word at the right has two syllables. Say the words, and check the spelling of the vowel sounds in the unstressed syllables.

1. Write the following list words correctly. Supply the letters that spell the unstressed vowel sounds.

barr—n	beac—n	summ—n
sen—te	summ—t	sull—n
cust—m	earn—st	reck—n
canv—ss	poll—n	patr—n
purch—se	cart—n	

2. Write the list words that end with **age** and **ege**.

3. Write the list words that end with **eon**.

bandage
barren
beacon
canvass
carton
college
custom
earnest
image
luncheon

patron
pigeon
pollen
purchase
reckon
senate
sullen
summit
summon
surgeon

30

Check the Spelling

a

1. Write the list words that have a double consonant.

2. Write the list words that end with the /j/ sound.

Check the Meaning

1. Write the list words that go with pictures **a, b,** and **c** at the right.

b

2. Copy the following sentences. Complete each sentence with a list word. Use the Speller Dictionary if you need help with any meanings.

a. He is a — of the arts.

b. She made an — effort to contact you.

c. The — in the mirror looked familiar.

d. I had enough money to — the radio.

3. When words are confused, a sentence sometimes has a ridiculous meaning. Copy the following sentences. Replace each word in heavy type with a list word that makes sense. Check with the Speller Dictionary if you need help with the meanings.

a. The **cartoon** of books was heavy.

b. Giving gifts is an old **costume.**

c. Her children attend **collage.**

d. The candidate will **canvas** for votes.

c

Can You Spell   every   minute   very

C   **Take the First Spelling Test**

Word Challenge

See if you can write a related word that will reveal the spelling of the unstressed vowel sound in the final syllable of each word below.

1. drama
2. method
3. palace
4. department

5. continent
6. moment
7. period
8. regular

Word Lore

At one time much of the southwest quarter of the United States was part of Mexico, and many of the people living there spoke Spanish. One of the results is that a large number of Spanish words have come into our language, most of them since the year 1800. Examples include **patio, fiesta, hacienda,** and **stampede.**

1. Each animal pictured at the right is labeled with its original Spanish name. See if you can write the words as we spell them today.

2. The following words are written with their original Spanish spellings. See if you can write each word as it is spelled today.

a. rancho
b. coyote
c. lazo

d. plaza
e. cañon
f. la reata

a. Spanish   borrico

b. Spanish   mestengo

Can You Spell

continental
departmental

dramatic
methodical

momentous
palatial

periodic
regularity

 E   **Take the Second Spelling Test**

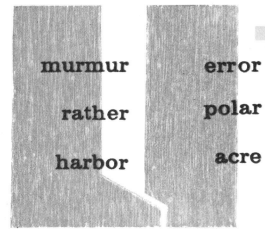

cougar   murmur   error

sulfur   rather   polar

slender   harbor   acre

? How many different spellings for the /ər/ ending can you discover in the words above?

A   The /ər/ Ending

Say the list words at the right. Check the spelling of the /ər/ ending in each word.

1. Write the list words that contain the /ər/ ending spelled with **—ar.**

2. Write the list words that contain the /ər/ ending spelled with **—er.**

3. Write the list words that contain the /ər/ ending spelled with **—or.**

actor
calendar
cedar
circular
director
governor
horror
interior
mediator
particular

plaster
radiator
register
saucer
senator
singular
splinter
superior
vapor
whether

33

Check the Spelling

Write the list word represented by each dictionary re-spelling below. Then underline the letters in each word that spell an unstressed vowel sound represented by /ə/. Check with the pronunciation key on page 115 and the word list at the right if you need help.

1. /kal′ ən dər/
2. /sėr′ kyə lər/
3. /guv′ ər nər/
4. /pər tik′ yə lər/
5. /rej′ ə stər/
6. /sen′ ə tər/

actor
calendar
cedar
circular
director
governor
horror
interior
mediator
particular
plaster
radiator
register
saucer
senator
singular
splinter
superior
vapor
whether

Check the Meaning

collie : dog : : trout : fish

Any expression or relationship such as the one above is called an **analogy.** Here is how to read an analogy.

A collie is a kind of dog, while a trout is a kind of fish.

OR

Collie is to dog as trout is to fish.

Write the list words that will complete the following analogies. Use the Speller Dictionary if you need help with any meanings.

1. flower : rose : : tree : —
2. sing : singer : : act : —
3. outside : inside : : exterior : —
4. city : state : : mayor : —
5. team : coach : : choir : —
6. two : one : : plural : —
7. triangle : triangular : : circle : —

Can You Spell   color   doctor   people

Take the First Spelling Test

Word Challenge

See if you can write a related word that will reveal the spelling of the /ər/ ending in each of the following words.

1. similar
2. author
3. polar
4. minor

5. senior
6. editor
7. familiar
8. popular

a

Word Lore

Many words that Americans have borrowed from the Spanish have a distinct Wild West flavor. The list below shows only a few examples.

bronco	calaboose	pronto	sombrero
buckaroo	desperado	rodeo	vamoose

1. See if you can write words from the list above that go with pictures **a, b,** and **c** at the right. Check with the Speller Dictionary if you need help with any meanings.

b

2. Copy the following sentences. See if you can complete each sentence with a word of Spanish origin. Choose your words from the list above.

a. The guard at the museum ordered us to —.

b. We had to leave the building —.

c. We raced past a statue of a bucking —.

c

Can You Spell

authority	familiarity	polarity	seniority
editorial	minority	popularity	similarity

E   **Take the Second Spelling Test**

35

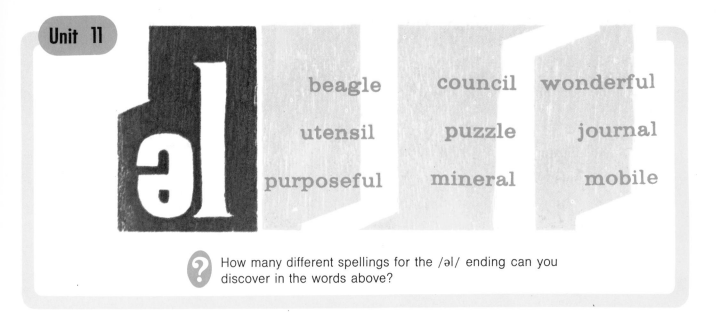

beagle   council   wonderful

utensil   puzzle   journal

purposeful   mineral   mobile

How many different spellings for the /əl/ ending can you discover in the words above?

A   The /əl/ Ending

Say the list words at the right. Check the spelling of the /əl/ ending in each word.

1. Write the list words that contain the /əl/ ending spelled with **−le.**

2. Write the list words that contain the /əl/ ending spelled with **−al.**

3. Write the list words that contain the /əl/ ending spelled with **−ul.**

4. Write the list word that contains the /əl/ ending spelled with **−il.**

5. Write the list words that contain the /əl/ ending spelled with **−ile.**

actual   historical
angle   missile
article   moral
carnival   reptile
cereal   rural
civil   steeple
consul   stumble
cycle   successful
feeble   tackle
grateful   useful

Check the Spelling

1. Write the list words represented by the dictionary respellings below. Underline the letter that spells the unstressed middle vowel sound in each word.

    a. /kär′ nə vəl/   b. /är′ tə kəl/

2. Write the list words that contain double consonants.

3. Write the list words that end with the suffix **–ful**.

4. Write the list word in which the vowel sound in the first syllable is spelled with **y**.

Check the Meaning

1. See if you can write the list words that complete riddles **a** and **b** under the pictures at the right.

2. Write the list word that matches each clue given below.

a. You can find a roller coaster and a Ferris wheel here.

b. Some people love to eat this for breakfast.

c. Watch your step, or you'll do this and fall.

d. An alligator is one of these.

e. It travels far and fast to reach its destination.

f. You might find this on top of a building.

g. This one lives in another country.

h. An area in the city could not be this.

a. Why is a football player usually good at math?

He can — any problem.

b. How did the mouse escape from the trap?

He figured all the —s.

Can You Spell   heard   quite   whole

Take the First Spelling Test

D Word Challenge

1. See if you can write a related word that will reveal the spelling of the /əl/ ending in each of the following words.

a. legal

b. symbol

c. metal

d. personal

e. normal

f. vital

g. national

h. idol

2. Use the Speller Dictionary to check the meanings of **idol** and **idle.** Then see if you can complete each sentence below with the correct homophone. Write each complete sentence on your paper.

a. All the factory workers were —.

b. That football player is the — of many young athletes.

Word Lore

The Spanish contributed a great number of place names to our country. Examples include **Los Angeles, Las Vegas,** and **San Antonio.** Other examples are shown on the map at the right.

1. Many place names of Spanish origin begin with **Los, Las,** or **San.** Using a map of the southwestern quarter of the United States, see how many cities beginning with **Los, Las,** and **San** you can find. Make a list of the cities.

2. Now, using a map of the southwestern quarter of the United States, make a list of other place names that you think are of Spanish origin.

Can You Spell

| idolatry | metallic | normality | symbolic |
| legality | nationality | personality | vitality |

E Take the Second Spelling Test

A   Review the List Words

Spelling Tip	The vowel sound in an unstressed syllable may be spelled many ways. The best way to learn words like the following is to use the study helps on page 5. cont**i**nent miss**i**le circul**a**r

1. Write the following list words correctly. Supply all the missing vowel letters.

a. crit—cize	j. rem—dy
b. abs—lute	k. civ—l
c. historic—l	l. band—ge
d. calend—r	m. circ—mstance
e. privil—ge	n. mediat—r
f. surg—n	o. cere—l
g. rept—le	p. cons—l
h. vap—r	q. spec—men
i. singul—r	r. wheth—r

absolute
admirable
bandage
calendar
cereal
circumstance
civil
consul
criticize
definite
historical
horizontal
magnet
mediator
melody
origin
privilege
remedy
reptile
singular
specimen
surgeon
vapor
whether

Spelling Tip	Sometimes a word that contains an unstressed vowel spelling has another form in which the spelling shows up clearly. Thinking of the related form will help you learn such words. com**e**dy → com**e**dian

2. The following words reveal the spelling of unstressed vowel sounds in six list words. Find the list words, and write each pair of related words on your paper.

a. original   c. magnetic   e. melodious

b. admire   d. define   f. horizon

More List Words to Review

1. Write the list words that have the following respellings. Underline all the double consonants. Check with the words at the right if you need help with any spellings.

a. /kol' ij/   e. /kan' vəs/

b. /mis' əl/   f. /hôr' ər/

c. /sum' it/   g. /sək ses' fəl/

d. /in' ə sənt/   h. /pol' ən/

2. Write the list words that name the objects in pictures **a** and **b**. Underline the letters that spell the vowel sound in the first syllable of each word.

a

b

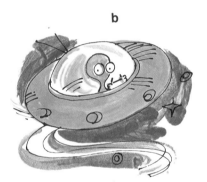

3. Write **courtesy, earnest,** and **purchase.** Underline the letter or letters that spell the vowel sound in the first syllable of each word.

4. Write **cycle** and **diagram.** Underline the letter that spells the /ī/ sound in each word.

5. Write **actual** and **fortunate.** Underline the letter that spells the /ch/ sound in each word.

6. Write **melodious** and **victorious.** Underline the letter that spells the /ē/ sound in each word.

7. Write **luncheon.** Underline the letters that spell the /ch/ sound. Write **parachute.** Underline the letters that spell the /sh/ sound.

actual
beacon
canvass
college
courtesy
cycle
diagram
earnest
fortunate
horror
innocent
luncheon
melodious
missile
parachute
pollen
purchase
saucer
successful
summit
victorious

Take the First Review Test

D Review the Challenging Words

1. See if you can write the month of the year represented by each dictionary respelling below. Then underline all the letters that spell the unstressed vowel sound represented by /ə/.

    a. /ok tō′ bər/   d. /ô′ gəst/

    b. /ā′ prəl/   e. /nō vem′ bər/

    c. /di sem′ bər/   f. /sep tem′ bər/

2. See if you can write a related word that will reveal the spelling of an unstressed vowel sound in each of the following words.

a. legal	k. economy
b. method	l. minor
c. drama	m. policy
d. palace	n. analyze
e. author	o. popular
f. vital	p. period
g. moment	q. senior
h. idol	r. specify
i. familiar	s. personal
j. atom	t. metal

palace—palatial

Can You Spell These Science Words

aerosol	fluoride	orbital
auricle	hemoglobin	planetary
chromosome	mandible	rocketry
electrolysis	measurement	skeletal
environment	molecule	velocity

E Take the Second Review Test

Why did the drummer take a chicken to the parade?

? **Why is a word like drumsticks called a compound word?**

He needed a pair of drumsticks.

 A **Compound Words**

All the words in the list at the right are compound words. Note that four of them are written as two words instead of one.

1. Write the compound words from the list that are written as single words.

2. Write the compound words from the list that are written as two separate words.

applesauce
bricklayer
copyright
drugstore
farewell
high school
nightmare
overcoat
parcel post
real estate

silverware
skyscraper
speedboat
spellbound
statesman
sunburn
tape recorder
touchdown
turnpike
undermine

Check the Spelling

a

1. Write the list words that contain a double consonant.

2. Write the list words that contain **gh.**

Check the Meaning

1. Pictures **a, b,** and **c** at the right are clues to three list words. See if you can find and write the words.

2. Write the list words that you could use to complete the following analogies. Use the Speller Dictionary if you need help with any meanings.

b

  a. invention : patent : : book : —

  b. bread : bakery : : medicine : —

  c. baseball : home run : : football : —

  d. stream : river : : street : —

  e. pipe : plumber : : brick : —

  f. arrival : hello : : departure : —

  g. medicine : illness : : ointment : —

  h. help : hinder : : support : —

  i. peanut : peanut butter : : apple : —

  j. sight : camera : : sound : —

  k. plate : knife : : china : —

  l. dean : college : : principal : —

c

Can You Spell   anything   awhile   everybody

C   Take the First Spelling Test

43

D   Word Challenge

Study the chart below to see if you can discover why each compound word has a double consonant.

> fis<u>h</u> + <u>h</u>ook → fis<u>hh</u>ook
>
> ea<u>r</u> + <u>r</u>ing → ea<u>rr</u>ing

a

Now see if you can apply the same pattern in forming the following compound words. Write each compound word.

1. news + stand
2. room + mate
3. night + time
4. book + keeper
5. head + dress
6. bath + house

Word Lore

Our language today contains a large number of compound words coined between the years 1600 and 1800. This was the time when English-speaking people were first settling in America, and they needed new words to name many of the new plants and animals that they found here.

b

1. Pictures **a, b,** and **c** at the right are clues to three compound words that Americans coined between 1600 and 1800. See if you can write the compound words.

2. The words below are clues to other compound words that Americans coined between 1600 and 1800. See if you can write the compound words.

    a. under + brush   b. cotton + wood

c

Can You Spell

bathhouse	earring	headdress	nighttime
bookkeeper	fishhook	newsstand	roommate

E   Take the Second Spelling Test

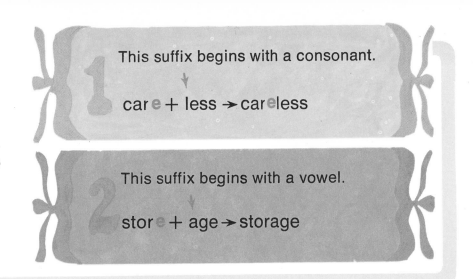

Unit 14

This suffix begins with a consonant.

car e + less → car e less

 What two patterns can you discover for adding suffixes to words that end with **e?**

This suffix begins with a vowel.

stor e + age → storage

A   **Suffixes and Final e**

Use the following words and suffixes to see what words you can write. When you finish, check your spellings against the list words at the right.

1. advertise + ment
2. examine + ing
3. circulate + ing
4. challenge + er
5. coarse + ness
6. insulate + ed
7. evaluate + ed
8. incorporate + ed
9. cultivate + ing
10. indicate + ed

11. rotate + ing
12. use + able
13. bruise + ed
14. assure + ed
15. assume + ed
16. sincere + ly
17. accuse + ed
18. explore + er
19. hesitate + ed
20. precise + ly

accused
advertisement
assumed
assured
bruised
challenger
circulating
coarseness
cultivating
evaluated

examining
explorer
hesitated
incorporated
indicated
insulated
precisely
rotating
sincerely
usable

B Check the Spelling

1. Write the list word represented by each dictionary respelling below. Check with the pronunciation key on page 115 and the word list at the right if you need help.

a. /in′ də kā′ tid/   e. /in kôr′ pə rā′ tid/

b. /chal′ ən jər/   f. /in′ sə lā′ tid/

c. /hez′ ə tā′ tid/   g. /sėr′ kyə lā′ ting/

d. /rō′ tā ting/   h. /kul′ tə vā′ ting/

2. Write the list words that contain double consonants.

Check the Meaning

Copy the following sentences. Complete each one with a list word. Use the Speller Dictionary if you need help with any meanings.

1. The committee — the new athletic program.

2. The lawn mower was rusty, but —.

3. The play began — at 8:00 P.M.

4. The space — walked on the moon.

5. We — appreciate your help.

6. The skater — her arm when she fell.

7. The doctor is — the X ray now.

8. My brother — me of eating his dessert.

9. I heard your — on the radio this morning.

accused
advertisement
assumed
assured
bruised
challenger
circulating
coarseness
cultivating
evaluated
examining
explorer
hesitated
incorporated
indicated
insulated
precisely
rotating
sincerely
usable

Can You Spell   coming   having   making

C Take the First Spelling Test

46

D Word Challenge

Study the chart below. See if you can discover a special pattern for adding **—able** and **—ous** to words that end with **ce** and **ge**.

> manage + able → manage<u>a</u>ble
>
> courage + ous → courage<u>ou</u>s
>
> notice + able → notic<u>ea</u>ble

Now see if you can apply the same pattern in adding **—able** or **—ous** to each of the following words. Write the words.

1. outrage + ous
2. replace + able
3. knowledge + able
4. pronounce + able
5. enforce + able
6. trace + able

1

Word Lore

Our language today contains a large number of compound words that Americans coined during the 1800's. Some examples follow.

headlight	chewing gum
motion pictures	storm door
roller skates	barbed wire

Note that all these compound words are names of inventions which were produced during that period.

2

Pictures **1, 2, 3,** and **4** are clues to four compound words that Americans coined during the 1800's. See if you can write the compound words.

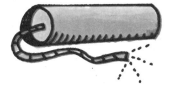

3

enforceable   knowledgeable   outrageous   replaceable
jackknife   noticeable   pronounceable   typewriter

4

E Take the Second Spelling Test

47

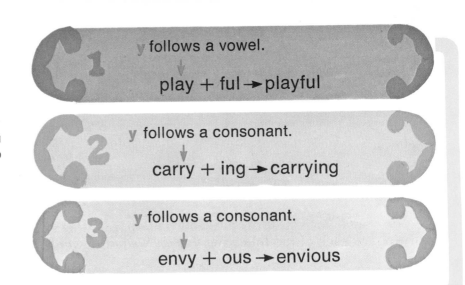

1   **y** follows a vowel.
↓
play + ful → playful

2   **y** follows a consonant.
↓
carry + ing → carrying

3   **y** follows a consonant.
↓
envy + ous → envious

? What three patterns can you discover for adding suffixes to words that end with **y?**

 A   **Suffixes and Final y**

Use the following words and suffixes to see what words you can write. When you finish, check your spellings against the list words at the right.

1. locality + es	11. emergency + es	*activities* *localities*
2. agency + es	12. chimney + s	*agencies* *modifying*
3. convey + ance	13. activity + es	*allergies* *occupying*
4. certify + ed	14. quality + es	*amplifying* *pulleys*
5. occupy + ing	15. satisfy + ing	*certified* *qualified*
6. security + es	16. specify + ed	*chimneys* *qualities*
7. modify + ing	17. community + es	*communities* *quantities*
8. pulley + s	18. amplify + ing	*conveyance* *satisfying*
9. quantity + es	19. allergy + es	*dismayed* *securities*
10. dismay + ed	20. qualify + ed	*emergencies* *specified*

Check the Spelling

1. Write the list words that are formed by adding suffixes to the following words.

       a. activity   d. emergency

       b. security   e. agency

       c. community   f. chimney

2. Write the list words that begin with **qu.**

Check the Meaning

1. See if you can write the list words that complete rhymes **a** and **b** under the pictures at the right.

2. Write the list words that you could use to replace the words in heavy type below. Use the Speller Dictionary if you need help with meanings.

  a. The team's record **discouraged** their coach.

  b. Mrs. Jordan invests in **stocks and bonds.**

  c. I called several employment **business offices.**

  d. These loudspeakers are **increasing** the sound.

  e. What **means of transportation** do you use most often?

  f. The recipe **told exactly** how much flour to use.

  g. The reporter interviewed people in two **regions.**

  h. Did you hire a **capable** plumber?

  i. Is this meat **guaranteed to be good?**

Can You Spell   always   buy   says

C
       Take the First Spelling Test

a. Gold spots upon my knees
Tell all about my —.

b. No excuses or denying.
My manners need some —.

49

Word Challenge

See what new words you can build by combining the following words and suffixes. Write each word.

1. journey + ed
2. annoy + ance
3. lucky + ly
4. employ + ment
5. rely + able

6. deny + al
7. library + an
8. enjoy + able
9. apply + ance
10. territory + al

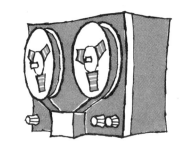

a. tape —

Word Lore

Our language today contains hundreds of compound words that Americans have coined since the year 1900.

1. Use the sentence clues below to discover four compound words that Americans have coined since 1900. Write each compound as one word.

a. This type of **fiber** contains **glass.**

b. This **boat** moves at a high **speed.**

c. Use this **board** instead of a **skate.**

d. Use this **light** to **search** at night.

b. aerosol —

2. Pictures **a, b,** and **c** at the right are clues to three more compound words that Americans have coined since 1900. Write each compound as two separate words.

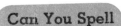

Can You Spell

annoyance	employment	journeyed	luckily
appliance	enjoyable	librarian	territorial

c. flying —

Take the Second Spelling Test

Here is how to decide when to double a final consonant before adding a suffix.

➡ The word must have one syllable or a stress on the final syllable.

➡ The word must have just one vowel before the final consonant.

➡ The suffix must begin with a vowel.

1 *stop* → *stopped*
2 *allot* → *allotted*

? Why do **stop** and **allot** double the final consonant before adding **-ed?**

Doubling Before Suffixes

1. Write the list words you can make by combining the following one-syllable words and suffixes.

   a. bob + ed   c. rob + ery

   b. quiz + es   d. scar + ed

2. Write the list words you can make by combining the following two-syllable words and suffixes.

   a. expel + ed   e. rebel + ed

   b. expel + ing   f. rebel + ion

   c. occur + ed   g. recur + ed

   d. occur + ence   h. recur + ent

bob
bobbed
expel
expelled
expelling
occur
occurred
occurrence
quiz
quizzes

rebel
rebelled
rebellion
recur
recurred
recurrent
rob
robbery
scar
scarred

Check the Spelling

1. Write the list words that begin with the prefix **ex−**.

2. Write the list words that begin with the prefix **re−**.

3. Write **rebellion.** Underline the letter that spells the /y/ sound.

Check the Meaning

1. Write the list words that go with the following meanings. Use the Speller Dictionary for any help you may need.

a. to happen, to take place   c. to dismiss, to drive out

b. to happen again, to repeat   d. a test, an examination

2. Copy the following sentences. Complete each sentence with a list word.

a. The burn on my arm left a tiny −.

b. She − for apples at the Halloween party.

c. The people − against the unfair tax.

d. Have you ever had a − dream?

e. Hobo Day is a yearly − at our school.

f. I have two − in science this week.

g. Why were those students − from school?

h. The police caught the thief after the −.

i. The accident − on the expressway.

Can You Spell   beginning   getting   swimming

Take the First Spelling Test

bob
bobbed
expel
expelled
expelling
occur
occurred
occurrence
quiz
quizzes
rebel
rebelled
rebellion
recur
recurred
recurrent
rob
robbery
scar
scarred

Word Challenge

See what new words you can build by combining the following words and suffixes. Write each word.

1. control + ed   4. propel + ing

2. transmit + ing   5. acquit + ed

3. remit + ed   6. equip + ing

Word Lore

Many of the compound words that Americans have coined are quite colorful. **Cowcatcher** and **crazy quilt** are two cases in point. **Cowcatcher** was first used by the early railroaders to name the front part of a train that cleared obstacles from the train's path. **Crazy quilt** was the name given to a quilt made of patches of different sizes and colors.

a. — writer

1. See if you can think of two colorful compound words to go with pictures **a** and **b** at the right. Write each compound as two separate words.

2. Three more colorful compound words appear in heavy type in the sentences below. See if you can write a meaning for each one. Check with the Speller Dictionary if you need help.

a. No one likes to play with a **roughneck**.

b. Did you **rubberneck** and push to see the movie star?

c. The fans were **crestfallen** when their team lost.

b. — meal

Can You Spell

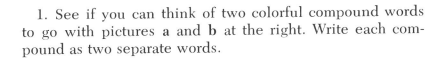

acquitted	crestfallen	propelling	roughneck
controlled	equipping	remitted	transmitting

         Take the Second Spelling Test

1 You don't double when the final consonant follows two vowels.

con-tain′→con-tained′

2 You don't double when the suffix begins with a consonant.

e-quip′→e-quip′ment

3 You don't double when the stress is on the first syllable.

trav′el→trav′eled

4 You don't double when the stress shifts to the first syllable when -**ence** is added.

con-fer′→con′fer-ence

? Do any of the words in color double the final consonant before adding the suffix? Why not?

A Adding Suffixes Without Doubling

Once you learn the rule for doubling a final consonant before adding a suffix, you have to be careful not to use it where it doesn't apply. For example, none of the list words at the right have a double consonant before the suffix. Use the chart above to discover the reasons why.

1. Write the list words that end with the —**ed** suffix.

2. Write the list words that end with the —**ence** suffix.

3. Write the list words that end with the —**ment** suffix.

allotment
attained
balloted
battered
canceled
commitment
concealed
difference
edited
labeled

marveled
merited
paneled
piloted
preference
reference
restrained
revealed
rumored
sponsored

Check the Spelling

1. Write each list word that contains a double consonant.

2. Write the list words that begin with the prefix **re−**.

Check the Meaning

a. prefer

1. Pictures **a**, **b**, and **c** at the right are clues to three of the list words. See if you can find and write the words.

2. Copy the second sentence in each pair below. Complete each sentence with a list word. Use the Speller Dictionary if you need help with any meanings.

a. We couldn't see the strings on the marionette.
   They had been well −.

b. The manuscript was ready for publication.
   It had been carefully −.

c. The Citizens' League paid all the team's expenses.
   They − the team.

b. pilot

d. The captain spotted the storm ahead.
   She − the ship to safety.

e. The news spread throughout the building.
   It was − that our visitors had arrived.

f. The temples were a wondrous sight.
   We − at their beauty.

g. The dancers gave a spectacular performance.
   They certainly − the talent award.

Can You Spell   nineteen   ninety   ninth

c. refer

Take the First Spelling Test

D   Word Challenge

See what new words you can write by combining the following words and suffixes.

1. refer + ee
2. infer + ence
3. benefit + ed
4. exclaim + ed
5. profit + able
6. forfeit + ed
7. attain + ment
8. cater + ing

Word Lore

People have been making up compound words just as long as English has been a language, and they are still doing it today. There is no reason why you can't join in the fun, too, if you want to.

1. Copy the following sentences. See what colorful compound word you can invent to complete each one.

a. If you can catch a **fish** with a **fishhook,** you might catch a **turtle** with a —.

b. If **hair** is smoothed with a **hairbrush,** a **beard** might be smoothed with a —.

c. If the **power** of **horses** is called **horsepower,** the **power** of **ants** could be called —.

2. See what colorful compound words you can invent to complete sentences **a** and **b** under the pictures at the right. Write the words.

a. The person who wins a first in the **camp** relay is the —.

b. A car accident that puts a dent in a **fender** is called a —.

Can You Spell

attainment	forfeited	inference	profitable
benefited	hairbrush	manpower	referee

E   Take the Second Spelling Test

56

Unit 18 Review and Evaluation

A   Review the List Words

Spelling Tip	Remember to drop final **e** before adding a suffix beginning with a vowel. use + able → usable

1. Write the list words you can make by combining the following words and suffixes.

a. accuse + ed   c. coarse + ness   e. bruise + ed

b. cultivate + ing   d. challenge + er   f. precise + ly

Spelling Tip	Remember to change final **y** to **i** before adding a suffix to a word like **carry**. EXCEPTION: Keep final **y** when adding a suffix beginning with **i**. carry + ed → carried carry + ing → carrying

2. Write the list words you can make by combining the following words and suffixes.

a. community + es   c. pulley + s   e. agency + es

b. amplify + ing   d. dismay + ed   f. satisfy + ing

Spelling Tip	Remember that words like **stop** and **allot** usually double the final consonant before adding a suffix beginning with a vowel.

3. Write the list words you can make by combining the following words and suffixes.

a. scar + ed   e. recur + ent   i. occur + ed

b. rebel + ed   f. cancel + ed   j. prefer + ence

c. commit + ment   g. expel + ing   k. rob + ery

d. restrain + ed   h. reveal + ed   l. panel + ed

accused
agencies
amplifying
bruised
canceled
challenger
coarseness
commitment
communities
cultivating
dismayed
expelling
occurred
paneled
precisely
preference
pulleys
rebelled
recurrent
restrained
revealed
robbery
satisfying
scarred

57

More List Words To Review

1. Write the list words that have the following respellings. Underline the letters that represent an unstressed vowel sound represented by /ə/. Check with the words at the right if you need any help with the spelling.

a. /ad′ vər tīz′ mənt/

b. /i mėr′ jən sēz/

c. /in kôr′ pə rā′ tid/

d. /sėr′ kyə lā′ ting/

e. /yü′ zə bəl/

f. /in′ sə lā′ tid/

g. /ə kėr′ əns/

h. /kwon′ tə tēz/

2. Write five list words that contain just one double consonant. Choose from the words at the right.

3. Write three compound words that are written as single words. Choose the compounds from the words at the right.

4. Write three compound words that are written as two separate words. Choose the compounds from the words at the right.

5. Write **preference** and **reference**. Underline the −ence suffix in each word.

6. Write **sincerely** and **precisely**. Underline the letter that comes before the −ly suffix in each word.

advertisement
allotment
assured
balloted
circulating
commitment
copyright
emergencies
incorporated
insulated
nightmare
occupying
occurrence
parcel post
precisely
preference
quantities
real estate
reference
silverware
sincerely
tape recorder
usable

Take the First Review Test

D **Review the Challenging Words**

1. Copy the following sentences. See if you can complete each one by adding **–ed** to the word in parentheses. Check the examples at the right if you need help.

a. The caravan (journey) to its destination.

b. Which player (forfeit) the game?

c. Was the defendant finally (acquit)?

d. The plants (benefit) from the rain yesterday.

e. Several guards (control) the joyous crowd.

2. See what words you can write by combining the following words and word parts. Check the examples at the right if you need help.

a. equip + ing
b. propel + ing
c. annoy + ance
d. room + mate
e. transmit + ing
f. pronounce + able
g. replace + able
h. library + an

i. enjoy + able
j. infer + ence
k. employ + ment
l. knowledge + able
m. lucky + ly
n. book + keeper
o. apply + ance
p. territory + al

Can You Spell These Language Words

abbreviation
auxiliary
capitalization
composition
conjunction

contraction
declarative
derivation
determiner
dictionary

exclamatory
parenthetical
pronunciation
quotation
vocabulary

E **Take the Second Review Test**

1

rattle + snake → rattlesnake
sun + burn → sunburn

AND

ear + ring → ea<u>r</u>ring
news + stand → news<u>s</u>tand

2

explore + er → explorer
rotate + ing → rotating

BUT

notice + able → notic<u>e</u>able
outrage + ous → outrag<u>e</u>ous

3

deny + ing → denying
display + ed → displayed

BUT

beauty + ful → beaut<u>i</u>ful
injury + ous → injur<u>i</u>ous

4

control + ed → controlled
prefer + ing → preferring

BUT

appeal + ing → appea<u>l</u>ing
refer + ee → ref<u>e</u>ree

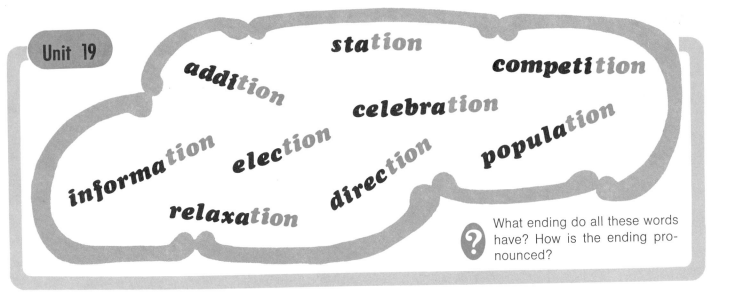

station

competition

addition

celebration

population

information

election

direction

relaxation

What ending do all these words have? How is the ending pronounced?

A The —tion Ending

All the list words at the right end with **—tion**. Say each word. Check to see whether the ending has the same pronunciation in each word.

1. Write the list words that are related to the words below. Note the changes that take place when the **—tion** ending is added to the words in each group.

a. alter, confirm, consider

b. examine, initiate, inspire, organize

c. except, exempt, protect, select

2. Write the remaining list words.

alteration
auction
confirmation
consideration
examination
exception
exemption
fiction
friction
function

ignition
initiation
inspiration
organization
portion
proportion
protection
reception
selection
solution

 Check the Spelling

a

1. Write the list words represented by the respellings below.

a. /ig nish′ ən/   e. /in′ spə rā′ shən/

b. /ôr′ gə nə zā′ shən/   f. /fungk′ shən/

c. /si lek′ shən/   g. /i nish′ ē ā′ shən/

d. /prə pôr′ shən/   h. /sə lü′ shən/

2. Write the list words that begin with the prefix **con−**.

3. Write the list words that begin with **ex−**.

b

Check the Meaning

1. Pictures **a,** **b,** and **c** at the right are clues to three list words. See if you can find and write a list word to go with each picture.

2. When words are confused, a sentence sometimes has a ridiculous meaning. Copy the following sentences. Replace each word in heavy type with a list word that makes sense. Check with the Speller Dictionary if you need help with any meanings.

a. Mr. Cole bought a lamp at the **action.**

b. I want a large **potion** of meat.

c. My new dress needs **alternation.**

d. A **deception** followed the wedding ceremony.

e. She learned judo for **projection.**

f. I enjoy watching science **friction** movies.

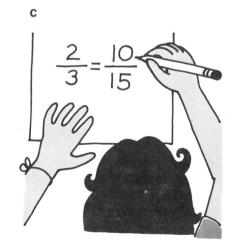

c

Can You Spell   answer   believe   enough

 Take the First Spelling Test

Word Challenge

See what new words you can write by adding the **−tion** ending to the following words.

a

1. transport + tion
2. fascinate + tion
3. civilize + tion
4. construct + tion
5. devote + tion
6. subscribe + tion
7. accuse + tion
8. qualify + tion

Word Lore

Our language today contains hundreds of words that Americans coined to name the hundreds of new inventions produced during the nineteenth century. Some examples are given in the list below.

bicycle	refrigerator	telephone
photograph	telegraph	X ray

b

1. Write the words that name the inventions in pictures **a, b,** and **c** at the right. Choose the words from the list above.

2. Copy the following sentences. See if you can complete each one with a word that names an invention of the nineteenth century. Choose the words from the list above.

a. Nan sent the message by −.

b. May I use your camera to take a − ?

c. I rode my − five miles yesterday.

c

Can You Spell

accusation	construction	fascination	subscription
civilization	devotion	qualification	transportation

E   **Take the Second Spelling Test**

? How are the endings in the words at the right the same, and how are they different?

1

***admis**sion*
***expan**sion*
***pen**sion*

2

***conclu**sion*
***confu**sion*
***excur**sion*

A

The —sion Ending

All the list words at the right end with —**sion**. Say the words. See if you can hear which words end with /shən/ and which ones end with /zhən/.

1. Write the list words that are related to the words below.

a. confuse
b. precise
c. tense
d. decide
e. proceed
f. expand
g. erode
h. transfuse
i. persuade
j. conclude
k. subvert
l. obsess
m. possess
n. admit
o. extend
p. progress

2. Write the remaining list words.

admission
conclusion
confusion
decision
erosion
excursion
expansion
extension
illusion
mansion

obsession
pension
persuasion
possession
precision
procession
progression
subversion
tension
transfusion

63

B Check the Spelling

1. Write the list words that contain double consonants.

2. Write the list words that begin with **ex–**.

3. Write the list words that begin with **con–**.

4. Write **persuasion.** Underline the letter that spells the /w/ sound.

Check the Meaning

Copy the following sentences. See if you can complete the sentences by writing list words that mean the same or almost the same as the words in heavy type. Check with the Speller Dictionary if you need help with any of the meanings.

1. The **mix-up** at the theater caused a lot of –.

2. **Stretching** my legs eased the –.

3. The **stately residence** is the governor's –.

4. A bird's **wing** is a useful –.

5. Her weekend **trip** to the mountains was a pleasant –.

6. The jury's **verdict** seemed a fair –.

7. **Property** was our most valuable –.

8. The circus **parade** was a colorful –.

9. **Accuracy** depends on the machine's –.

10. The strange **sight** was an optical –.

admission
conclusion
confusion
decision
erosion
excursion
expansion
extension
illusion
mansion
obsession
pension
persuasion
possession
precision
procession
progression
subversion
tension
transfusion

Can You Spell   ache   early   instead

C Take the First Spelling Test

D   Word Challenge

a

See what new words you can write by adding the **−sion** ending to the following words.

1. omit + sion
2. divide + sion
3. succeed + sion
4. submit + sion
5. provide + sion
6. permit + sion
7. suspend + sion
8. collide + sion
9. discuss + sion
10. commit + sion

Word Lore

b

During the twentieth century thousands of new words were added to our language as more and more new inventions appeared. **Transistor, aqualung,** and **superhighway** are only a few examples of the thousands of new words that Americans have coined since 1900.

1. The six words listed below name more inventions of the twentieth century. See if you can find and write a word to name each invention in pictures **a, b, c,** and **d** at the right.

c

bulldozer	parachute	television
helicopter	roller coaster	thermos

2. Copy the following sentences. See if you can complete each one with a word that names an invention of the twentieth century. Choose the words from the list in exercise 1.

a. Each skydiver was equipped with a −.

b. Felicia is watching her favorite − program.

d

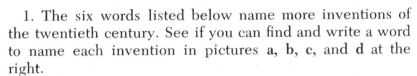

Can You Spell

collision	omission	provision	succession
commission	permission	submission	suspension

E   Take the Second Spelling Test

gener**ous** preci**ous** courage**ous**
marvel**ous** suspici**ous** gorge**ous**

? What is the chief problem in learning to spell words like these?

A The —ous Ending

All the list words at the right end with **—ous.** The **—ous** ending doesn't usually cause a spelling problem, but the letters that come before **—ous** sometimes do. Say the list words, and decide which words have unexpected spellings that you think might cause you trouble.

1. Write the list words in which the following spellings occur before **—ous.**

a. The **i** spelling of the /ē/ sound.

b. The **ci** spelling of the /sh/ sound.

c. The **ge** spelling of the /j/ sound.

d. The **t** spelling of the /ch/ sound.

2. Write the remaining list words.

advantageous
courageous
curious
delicious
enormous
furious
glorious
gracious
humorous
industrious

jealous
mysterious
numerous
obvious
previous
spacious
tedious
tremendous
vicious
virtuous

Check the Spelling

a

See if you can write the list word that is related to each of the following words.

1. mystery
2. virtue
3. space
4. industry
5. glory

6. advantage
7. fury
8. courage
9. humor
10. grace

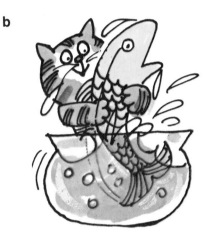

Check the Meaning

1. Pictures **a**, **b**, and **c** at the right are clues to three of the list words. See if you can find and write a list word to go with each picture.

b

Words that have opposite meanings are called **antonyms.**

2. Copy the following sentences. See if you can complete each one with a list word that is an antonym for the word in heavy type. Check with the Speller Dictionary if you need help with any meanings.

a. The **small** error cost an — amount to correct.

b. **Few** people have — pets.

c. The **serious** speech ended on a — note.

d. I met the **next** speaker at a — meeting.

e. The **lazy** boy grew to be an — man.

f. You were very **rude** to that — clerk.

g. The **narrow** walkway opened into a — courtyard.

c

Can You Spell   none   read   tear

C   **Take the First Spelling Test**

67

Word Challenge

Copy the following sentences. Complete each one by adding the **—ous** ending to the word in parentheses.

1. I am (envy) of your musical talent.

2. My sister is very (adventure).

3. Is too little sleep (injury) to one's health?

4. There's a (continue) stream of cars on this road.

5. This hat looks (ridicule) on me.

6. Our committee is a (harmony) group.

Word Lore

Some of the newest words in our language have to do with the exploration of space. **Retro-rockets** and **lift-off** are typical examples of new words that Americans have coined to talk about space and space exploration.

The four words in heavy type below deal with space and space exploration. Use the Speller Dictionary to find out what each word means. Then write the definitions on your paper.

1. A **booster vehicle** launched the spacecraft.

2. The spacecraft is now at its **apogee.**

3. How far from the earth is the spacecraft's **perigee?**

4. A **laser** can cut through hard materials.

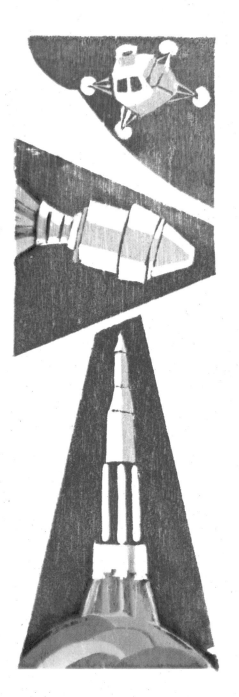

Can You Spell

adventurous	continuous	harmonious	perigee
apogee	envious	injurious	ridiculous

E   **Take the Second Spelling Test**

1

allowance
performance
reliance

2

evidence
independence
patience

 Why do the endings in words like these sometimes present a spelling problem?

A   —ance or —ence?

Say the list words at the right. Note the sound and the spelling of the final ending in each word.

1. Write the list words that end with **—ance.**

2. Write the list words that end with **—ence.**

allowance
appearance
assurance
attendance
brilliance
confidence
dependence
evidence
excellence
experience

fragrance
ignorance
independence
innocence
insurance
obedience
patience
performance
reliance
residence

Check the Spelling

See if you can write the list word that is related to each of the following words. When you have finished, check the spelling with the list words at the right.

1. resident
2. reliant
3. confident
4. attendant
5. innocent

6. evident
7. obedient
8. ignorant
9. brilliant
10. dependent

allowance
appearance
assurance
attendance
brilliance
confidence
dependence
evidence
excellence
experience
fragrance .
ignorance
independence
innocence
insurance
obedience
patience
performance
reliance
residence

Check the Meaning

Copy the second sentence in each pair below. Complete the sentence with a list word that is related to the word in heavy type in the first sentence.

1. I will **allow** you two dollars every week.
   Two dollars is your weekly —.

2. When will the jury **appear?**
   We are waiting for their —.

3. The man wants to **insure** his speedboat.
   The — for the boat will be expensive.

4. The orchestra will **perform** here next week.
   It is their first public —.

5. Vanessa can **excel** in all water sports.
   Her diving — is unmatched.

Can You Spell   because   cousin   hospital

Take the First Spelling Test

D   Word Challenge

Study the examples at the right to discover the relation between words ending in **—ant** or **—ent** and words ending in **—ance** or **—ence.** Then see if you can write the **—ance** or **—ence** form for each word below.

1. intelligent
2. arrogant
3. competent

4. diligent
5. radiant
6. negligent

1

fragra̱nt → fragra̱nce
tolera̱nt → tolera̱nce

2

evide̱nt → evide̱nce
patie̱nt → patie̱nce

Word Lore

Between 1830 and 1860 Americans invented a number of colorful words that were not related at all to any previously known words. Some of these words, like **shebang** and **rumpus,** are still used today. Below is a list of six more colorful words you may have heard or even used yourself.

caboodle	conniption	scrumptious
cahoots	rip-roaring	shindig

1. See if you can write the colorful words from the list above that complete sentences **a** and **b** under the pictures at the right. Check with the Speller Dictionary if you need help with the meanings.

2. Copy the following sentences. See if you can complete each one with a colorful word from the list above. Use the Speller Dictionary if you need any help.

a. This turkey sandwich is really —.

b. Sam had a — when he saw his damaged car.

a. It was a big —.

Can You Spell

arrogance	competence	intelligence	radiance
cahoots	diligence	negligence	shindig

E   Take the Second Spelling Test

b. They are in —.

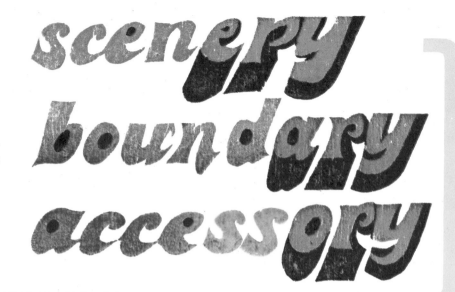

? What is the chief spelling problem in trying to learn words like these?

A   —ary, —ery, or —ory?

Say the list words at the right. Note the sound and spelling of each ending.

1. Write the list words that end with —ary.

2. Write the list words that end with —ery.

3. Write the list words that end with —ory.

accessory
anniversary
archery
artery
boundary
category
celery
contrary
embroidery
flattery

gallery
honorary
imaginary
literary
military
misery
ordinary
salary
scenery
summary

Check the Spelling

1. Write the list word represented by each dictionary respelling below. Then underline all the letters that spell the vowel sound represented by /ə/.

a

a. /lit′ ə rer′ ē/   d. /on′ ə rer′ ē/

b. /kat′ ə gôr ē/   e. /an′ ə vėr′ sər ē/

c. /mil′ ə ter′ ē/   f. /i maj′ ə ner′ ē/

2. Write the list words that contain double consonants.

Check the Meaning

b

1. Pictures **a, b,** and **c** at the right are clues to three of the list words. See if you can find and write the words.

2. Write the list words that you could use to replace the words in heavy type below. Use the Speller Dictionary if you need help with any of the meanings.

a. Who did the **stitchwork** on your shirt?

b. We enjoyed the gorgeous mountain **landscape.**

c. I read a **condensed version** of that novel.

d. Fred's ideas are **completely counter** to mine.

e. Where is the **border line** between the two farms?

f. The wealthy family lived in a very **common** home.

g. Which **vessel** carries blood directly from the heart?

c

h. We tried to lessen the **distress** of the flood victims.

Can You Spell   good-bye   o'clock   tonight

C   ### Take the First Spelling Test

D — Word Challenge

See what new words you can write by combining the following words and word endings.

1. custom + ary
2. transit + ory
3. element + ary
4. station + ery
5. legend + ary
6. moment + ary

a. <u>A</u>bsent <u>W</u>ith<u>o</u>ut <u>L</u>eave

Word Lore

Our language contains a number of words called **acronyms**— words formed by combining the first one or two letters of other words. For example, **scuba** is an acronym formed by combining letters in the words <u>s</u>elf-<u>c</u>ontained <u>u</u>nderwater <u>b</u>reathing <u>a</u>pparatus. **NASA** is also an acronym formed from the full name of the <u>N</u>ational <u>A</u>eronautics and <u>S</u>pace <u>A</u>dministration.

1. See if you can write acronyms for the words that go with pictures **a, b,** and **c** at the right.

2. See what acronyms you can write for each of the following groups of words.

a. <u>s</u>ound <u>n</u>avigation <u>a</u>nd <u>r</u>anging

b. <u>r</u>adio <u>d</u>etecting <u>a</u>nd <u>r</u>anging

c. <u>c</u>ontrol of <u>e</u>lectromagnetic <u>r</u>adiation

d. <u>Z</u>one <u>I</u>mprovement <u>P</u>lan (Code)

b. <u>T</u>ake <u>O</u>ff <u>P</u>ounds <u>S</u>ensibly

Can You Spell

conelrad	elementary	momentary	stationery
customary	legendary	radar	transitory

E — Take the Second Spelling Test

c. <u>I</u>nternational <u>Po</u>lice

Unit 24 Review and Evaluation

A

Review the List Words

Spelling Tip	The words in each pair below often cause a spelling problem because the endings have the same pronunciation but different spellings.

	1	2	3
	excep<u>tion</u>	allow<u>ance</u>	bound<u>ary</u>
	man<u>sion</u>	resid<u>ence</u>	scen<u>ery</u>

accessory
advantageous
auction
confirmation
courageous
delicious
embroidery
erosion
exemption
extension
gallery
ignorance
industrious
initiation
jealous
obedience
obsession
possession
progression
reliance
spacious
summary
tremendous
virtuous

1. Write the list words represented by the dictionary re-spellings below. Check with the words at the right if you need help with any spellings.

a. /pə zesh′ ən/

b. /i nish′ ē ā′ shən/

c. /ig′ nər əns/

d. /sum′ ər ē/

e. /gal′ ər ē/

f. /ō bē′ dē əns/

g. /ôk′ shən/

h. /prə gresh′ ən/

i. /ri lī′ əns/

j. /kon′ fər mā′ shən/

k. /ak ses′ ər ē/

l. /i rō′ zhən/

m. /em broi′ dər ē/

n. /əb sesh′ ən/

o. /eg zemp′ shən/

p. /ek sten′ shən/

Spelling Tip	The —ous ending seldom causes a spelling problem, but the letters that come before —ous sometimes do. The best way to learn to spell words like these is to use the study helps on page 5.

	pre<u>vi</u>ous	vi<u>ci</u>ous

2. The list at the right contains eight words that end with —ous. Find the words, and write them on your paper.

1. Write the list word represented by each respelling below. Underline the letters that spell an unstressed vowel sound represented by /ə/. Check with the words at the right if you need any help with the spelling.

a. /kat′ ə gôr′ ē/   e. /in′ spə rā′ shən/

b. /prə pôr′ shən/   f. /i maj′ ə ner′ ē/

c. /ôr′ gə nə zā′ shən/   g. /rez′ ə dəns/

d. /in′ di pen′ dəns/   h. /ôrd′ ən er′ ē/

2. Write four list words that contain a double consonant. Choose from the words at the right.

3. Write **scenery** and **honorary.** Underline the silent letter in the first syllable of each word.

4. Write **insurance.** Underline the letter that spells the /sh/ sound. Write **virtuous.** Underline the letter that spells the /ch/ sound.

5. Write **patience** and **gracious.** Underline the two letters that spell the /sh/ sound in each word.

6. Write **persuasion.** Underline the letter that spells the /w/ sound. Write **brilliance.** Underline the letter that spells the /y/ sound.

anniversary
brilliance
category
excellence
gracious
honorary
imaginary
independence
innocence
inspiration
insurance
ordinary
organization
patience
persuasion
proportion
residence
scenery
virtuous

C   **Take the First Review Test**

76

D Review the Challenging Words

1. Copy the following sentences. See if you can complete each one by adding **–tion** to the word in parentheses.

a. Can you explain Meg's (fascinate) with this movie?

b. Is there any truth to Derrick's (accuse)?

c. This book describes Greek (civilize).

d. I renewed my (subscribe) to the newspaper.

e. An inspector checked the (construct) of the house.

2. See what words you can write by combining the following words and suffixes.

a. element + ary

b. envy + ous

c. collide + sion

d. ridicule + ous

e. submit + sion

f. suspend + sion

g. station + ery

h. continue + ous

i. provide + sion

j. adventure + ous

k. legend + ary

l. custom + ary

m. transit + ory

n. harmony + ous

o. omit + sion

p. divide + sion

+ary
+ous
+tion
+sion
+ery

Can You Spell These Science Words

adaptation	conduction	ionization
aspiration	differentiation	malocclusion
cell division	diffusion	polarization
coagulation	dispersion	refraction
cohesion	dissociation	revolution

E Take the Second Review Test

? What information do the dictionary entries give about the origins of the words **tongue, reign, scalp,** and **private?**

tongue /tung/ *n.* **1.** An organ of speech. *The tongue of a human being is very flexible.* **2.** The spoken language of a people. **3.** The power of speech. [Old English *tunge*]

Tongue was originally an Old English word.

reign /rān/ *v.* To rule; to prevail. *How long did Queen Victoria of England reign?* [French *regne*]

Reign came into English from French.

scalp /skalp/ *n.* The skin on the top and back of the human head, usually covered with hair. *The hairdresser massaged my scalp before she washed my hair.* [Scandinavian *skalpr*]

Scalp came into English from Scandinavian.

private /prī′ vit/ *adj.* **1.** Not open to the public. *She attends a private school.* **2.** Secret. [Latin *privatus*]

Private was originally a Latin word.

A   Word Origins

Most words have a history, and most dictionaries document the history in an abbreviated form somewhere in the entry. The Speller Dictionary gives the history of each list word at the right. Look up each word to find its origin.

1. Write the list words that were originally Old English words.

2. Write the list words that came into English from Scandinavian.

3. Write the list words that came into English from French.

4. Write the list words that came into English from Latin.

blossom
culture
custody
emerald
endure
fleet
icy
marine
oath
pyramid

reindeer
scorch
singe
skull
smother
sponge
thirst
thrift
trustee
vanish

B   Check the Spelling

1. Write the list words represented by the respellings at the right. Underline all the letters that spell an unstressed vowel sound represented by /ə/.

2. Write **custody** and **trustee.** Underline the letter or letters that spell the /ē/ sound at the end of each word.

3. Write **pyramid** and **thirst.** Underline the letter that spells the vowel sound before the **r** in each word.

4. Write **culture** and **scorch.** Underline the letter or letters that spell the /ch/ sound in each word.

5. Write **smother** and **sponge.** Underline the letter that spells the /u/ sound in each word.

6. Write **reindeer.** Underline the letters that spell the /ā/ sound.

a. /mə rēn′/
b. /blos′ əm/
c. /em′ ər əld/
d. /pir′ ə mid/
e. /kus′ tə dē/

Check the Meaning

Copy the following sentences. Complete each sentence with a list word. Check with the Speller Dictionary if you need any help with meanings.

1. This dirt will — in seconds.

2. Whales and sharks are — animals.

3. Did the campers — the fire with sand?

4. We found a boar's — in the cave.

5. The witness testified under —.

Can You Spell   country   often   tired

C   Take the First Spelling Test

Word Challenge

Homophones are words that have the same pronunciation but different spellings and different meanings. Some examples include **fair** and **fare, waist** and **waste,** and **break** and **brake.**

1. Copy the following sentences. Complete each sentence with the correct one of the two homophones given in parentheses. Use the Speller Dictionary if you need help with meanings.

   a. (plain, plane) The explanation Debra gave was —.

   b. (all ready, already) We have, — packed our suitcases.

   c. (counsel, council) The lawyer will — us.

2. Each picture at the right could be labeled with one of the two homophones under it. Write the homophones you could use to label the pictures.

a. council or counsel?

Word Lore

Exploring the origins of words often turns up some surprises. The word **onion,** for example, began as the Latin word **unio,** which meant "a pearl." Does an onion look like a pearl to you? Have you ever heard of a pearl onion?

See if you can write the words that have the word origins on the left. Choose the words from the list in the box.

1. Greek **krystallos,** ice

2. French **brimbe,** bread offered to a beggar

3. Italian **ballotta,** a little ball

| ballot |
| bribe |
| crystal |

b. plain or plane?

Can You Spell

| ballot | council | plain | waist |
| crystal | counsel | plane | waste |

Take the Second Spelling Test

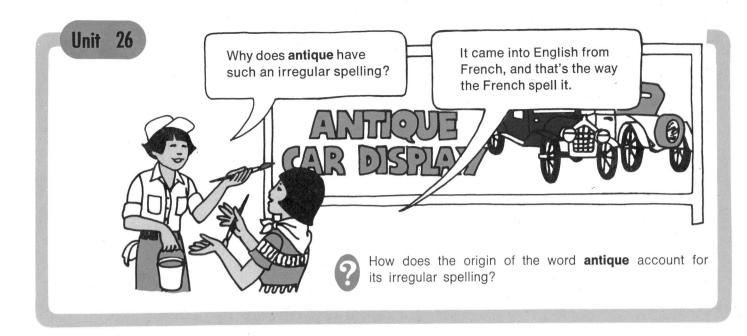

A   Word Origins and Spelling

All the list words at the right came into English from other languages, and most of them have the same or nearly the same spelling as they had in the original languages. This is the reason why so many of them have irregular spellings. See if you can write the list words that have the origins below.

1. French **amateur**
2. Greek **gymnasion**
3. Latin **agricultura**
4. Italian **spaghetti**
5. Latin **aquarius**
6. French **cocon**
7. Greek **bakterion**
8. Hindu **champo**
9. French **oxygène**
10. Czech **robota**
11. French **plateau**
12. Latin **geologia**
13. French **carrière**
14. Italian **all'erta**

agriculture
alert
amateur
aquarium
awkward
bacteria
career
cocoon
frankfurter
geology
gymnasium
hamburger
kindergarten
oxygen
plateau
robot
sauerkraut
shampoo
spaghetti
volcano

Check the Spelling

1. Write **career** and **cocoon.** Underline the letter that spells the /ə/ sound in the first syllable of each word.

2. Write **plateau** and **volcano.** Underline the letter or letters that spell the /ō/ sound at the end of each word.

3. Write **amateur** and **sauerkraut.** Underline the vowel spellings in each word.

4. Write **aquarium** and **awkward.** Underline the letters that spell /kw/ in each word.

5. Write **kindergarten.** Underline the three letters that spell the last syllable. Write **spaghetti.** Underline the double consonant.

Check the Meaning

Write the list word you could use to complete each of the following analogies. Use the Speller Dictionary if you need help with any meanings.

1. automobile : industry : : corn : —

2. animal : horse : : microorganism : —

3. teeth : toothpaste : : hair : —

4. bird : cage : : fish : —

5. animal : biology : : earth : —

6. metal : steel : : gas : —

7. master : apprentice : : professional : —

Can You Spell   chord   their   there

C   **Take the First Spelling Test**

agriculture
alert
amateur
aquarium
awkward
bacteria
career
cocoon
frankfurter
geology
gymnasium
hamburger
kindergarten
oxygen
plateau
robot
sauerkraut
shampoo
spaghetti
volcano

Word Challenge

1. Copy the following sentences. Complete each sentence with the correct one of the two homophones given in parentheses. Use the Speller Dictionary if you need help with meanings.

a. (strait, straight) The ship entered the — at dawn.

b. (cereal, serial) This is the last episode of the —.

c. (profit, prophet) We can all — from your experience.

d. (cents, sense) Joan's common — told her what to do.

2. Each picture at the right could be labeled with one of the two homophones under it. Write the homophones you could use to label the pictures.

Word Lore

The origins of **sauerkraut, kindergarten,** and **spaghetti** are interesting. **Sauerkraut** means "sour cabbage" in German. **Kindergarten** means "a children's garden" in German. **Spaghetti** means "little strings" in Italian.

See if you can write the words that have the word origins on the left. Choose the words from the list in the box.

1. French **pensée,** thought
2. Greek **tragoidia,** goat song
3. Spanish **armadillo,** little armed one
4. Old English **daegeseage,** day's eye
5. Malayan **oran utan,** wild man

| armadillo |
| daisy |
| orangutan |
| pansy |
| tragedy |

a. cereal or serial?

Can You Spell

| armadillo | profit | sense | strait |
| cents | prophet | serial | tragedy |

b. cents or sense?

Take the Second Spelling Test

Unit 27

LATIN BASE	GENERAL MEANING	EXAMPLE
audi	hear	audible
loqu	talk	soliloquy
nom	name	nominee
pon, pos	put, place	position
vid, vis	see	provide

 What other words can you think of that contain these Latin bases?

A   Words from Latin

All the list words at the right contain Latin bases from the chart. See if you can decide what bases the words contain. Hint: The base in **preview** is **vid,** and the base in **depot** is **pon.**

1. Write the list words that contain the Latin base **pon** or **pos.**

2. Write the list words that contain the Latin base **vid** or **vis.**

3. Write the list words that contain the Latin base **audi.**

4. Write the list words that contain the Latin base **nom.**

5. Write the list words that contain the Latin base **loqu.**

audience
preposition
loquacious
visible
depot
supervision
audition
visualize
expose
nominal

preview
nominate
eloquent
colloquial
auditorium
denominator
postpone
evidently
transpose
visual

B Check the Spelling

1. Write the list words represented by the dictionary respellings at the right. Underline all the letters that spell an unstressed vowel sound represented by /ə/. Use the pronunciation key on page 115 if you need help with any symbols.

2. Write **visual** and **visualize.** Underline the letter that spells the /zh/ sound in each word.

3. Write **loquacious.** Underline the letters that spell the /sh/ sound. Write **depot.** Underline the silent letter.

a. /ô′ də tôr′ ē əm/

b. /nom′ ə nəl/

c. /prep′ ə zish′ ən/

d. /di nom′ ə nā′ tər/

e. /ô′ dē əns/

f. /kə lō′ kwē əl/

g. /el′ ə kwənt/

h. /nom′ ə nāt/

Check the Meaning

1. Write the list words that go with the definitions below. Check with the Speller Dictionary if you need help.

a. to name a candidate

b. to see in the mind

c. a hearing to test a performer

d. in name only

e. capable of being seen

f. well-spoken

2. Write the list words that you could use to replace the words in heavy type below. Check with the Speller Dictionary if you need help.

a. Sometimes Andy is too **talkative.**

b. This story is written in a **conversational** style.

c. I can meet Rosa at the **train station.**

d. Did you **interchange** these two numbers?

e. This is **clearly** the wrong address.

Can You Spell   among   friend   meant

C   Take the First Spelling Test

85

Word Challenge

1. Copy the following sentences. Complete each sentence with the correct one of the two homophones given in parentheses. Use the Speller Dictionary if you need help with any meanings.

   a. (guest, guessed) I invited Jim to be my dinner —.

   b. (fur, fir) The leather gloves were lined with —.

   c. (buoy, boy) My cousin is the — in the blue shirt.

2. Each picture at the right could be labeled with one of the two homophones under it. Write the homophones you could use to label the pictures.

Word Lore

Some word origins seem to be quite logical. The word **ambulance,** for example, comes from the French **hopital ambulant,** a phrase meaning "a walking hospital." Do you agree that a walking hospital is a logical name for an ambulance?

The following words have origins that make good sense once you stop to think about them. Study the origins yourself to see if you agree.

1. **Companion** goes back to the Latin **com,** with + **panis,** bread.

2. **Comrade** goes back to the Spanish **camarada,** a roommate.

3. **Aviator** goes back to the Latin **avis,** a bird.

4. **Slogan** goes back to the Gaelic **sluagh-ghairm,** a battle cry.

a. fir or fur?

b. boy or buoy?

Can You Spell

ambulance	buoy	comrade	fur
aviator	companion	fir	slogan

E **Take the Second Spelling Test**

What other words can you think of that contain these Latin and Greek bases?

1

LATIN BASE	GENERAL MEANING	EXAMPLE
mit, miss	send	mission
scrib, script	write	scribble
tract	pull, draw	tractor
ven	come	convention

2

GREEK BASE	GENERAL MEANING	EXAMPLE
bio	life	biology
nym	name	homonym
poli	city	police
sphere	globe	atmosphere

A   Latin and Greek Bases

All the list words at the right contain Latin or Greek bases from the chart. Say the words. See if you can decide what the base in each word is.

1. Write the list words that contain the following Latin bases.

    a. mit, miss   c. tract

    b. scrib, script   d. ven

2. Write the list words that contain the following Greek bases.

    a. bio   c. poli

    b. nym   d. sphere

traction
hemisphere
convene
policy
prevention
postscript
sphere
transcribe
synonyms
dismissal

biography
amphibian
stratosphere
antonyms
detract
antibiotic
intervention
attract
politics
remittance

Check the Spelling

1. Write the list words in which **ph** spells the /f/ sound.

2. Write the list words in which **y** spells the /i/ sound.

3. Write **hemisphere** and **stratosphere.** Underline the letter that spells the /ə/ sound in the middle syllable of each word.

4. Write the list words that contain double consonants.

Check the Meaning

1. Copy the following sentences. See if you can complete each one with a list word. Check with the Speller Dictionary if you need help with any meanings.

a. This — is Carol's final payment for her bicycle.

b. Our meeting will — at two o'clock.

c. A salamander is an —.

d. Gordon wrote a — to his letter.

e. The doctor used an — to treat the disease.

f. A basketball is a —.

2. Write the list words that have the definitions below. Check with the Speller Dictionary if you need help with any meanings.

a. to draw attention from

b. the act of coming between

c. the story of a person's life

d. a plan of action

e. to make a copy of

f. half of a sphere

amphibian
antibiotic
antonyms
attract
biography
convene
detract
dismissal
hemisphere
intervention
policy
politics
postscript
prevention
remittance
sphere
stratosphere
synonyms
traction
transcribe

Can You Spell   guess   just   where

Take the First Spelling Test

Word Challenge

1. Words like **ally** and **alley** are often confusing. Copy the following sentences. See if you can complete each sentence by writing the correct one of the two words given in parentheses. Use the Speller Dictionary if you need help with meanings.

a. (alley, ally) The truck was wider than the —.

b. (clothes, cloths) He stuffed the puppet with old —.

c. (decent, descent) It was — of you to defend her.

d. (aboard, abroad) I was the last one to go — the plane.

2. Each picture at the right could be labeled with one of the two confusing words under it. Write the words you could use to label the pictures.

a. cloths or clothes?

Word Lore

Some words have origins far removed from the meanings of the words today. The word **celery,** for example, goes back to a Greek word that meant "parsley." The word **lace** goes back to a Latin word that meant "a noose."

See if you can write the words that have the word origins on the left. Choose the words from the list in the box.

1. Old English **godsibb,** a godparent

2. Hawaiian **uku lele,** a leaping flea

3. Latin **buculus,** a little cow

4. Latin **musculus,** a little mouse

| bugle |
| gossip |
| muscle |
| ukulele |

b. decent or descent?

Can You Spell

| aboard | alley | decent | gossip |
| abroad | ally | descent | ukulele |

 E   **Take the Second Spelling Test**

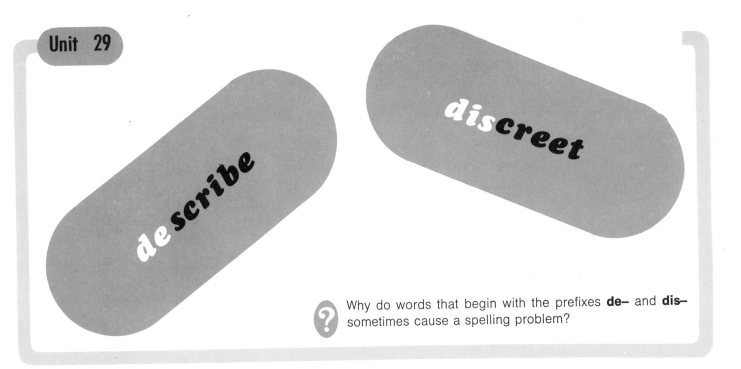

Why do words that begin with the prefixes **de–** and **dis–** sometimes cause a spelling problem?

 A   **Two Problem Prefixes**

Say the list words at the right, and check the spelling of the prefix in each word.

1. Write the list words that begin with the prefix **de–**.

2. Write the list words that begin with the prefix **dis–**.

disgust

despise

deceased

disguise

despair

disposition

discuss

deprive

disperse

deflate

destination

discreet

distribution

decisive

description

distribute

discretion

destruction

disease

declaration

Check the Spelling

a

1. Write the list words formed by adding the prefix **de–** to a base that begins with **s.**

2. See if you can write the list word that is related to each of the following words.

        a. distribute   c. declare

        b. describe   d. decide

Check the Meaning

1. Pictures **a** and **b** at the right are clues to two of the list words. See if you can find and write the list word that goes with each picture.

2. Write the list words that will complete the following analogies. Check with the Speller Dictionary if you need help with any meanings.

b

    a. departure : starting point : : arrival : —

    b. awake : asleep : : alive : —

    c. color : painting : : word : —

    d. give : reward : : take : —

    e. summer : winter : : hope : —

    f. building : breakup : : construction : —

    g. wealth : poverty : : health : —

    h. love : hate : : respect : —

    i. gather : collect : : scatter : —

Can You Spell   raise   ready   said

Take the First Spelling Test

Word Challenge

1. Copy the following sentences. Complete each sentence by writing the correct one of the two words given in parentheses. Use the Speller Dictionary if you need help with meanings.

 a. (quiet, quite) He was — unaware of our presence.

 b. (breathe, breath) I took a deep — before I began.

 c. (advice, advise) The counselor gave me some good —.

 d. (lose, loose) There are several — pages in this book.

2. The picture at the right could be labeled with one of the two confusing words under it. Write the word you could use to label the picture.

loose or lose?

Word Lore

Here are some more word origins that may surprise you.

Climax goes back to the Greek **klimax,** which meant "a ladder."

Camera goes back to the Latin **camera,** which meant "a large room."

Chapel goes back to the Latin **cappa,** which meant "a cape."

See if you can write the English words that have these origins.

 1. Greek **agonia,** a contest

 2. Latin **crispus,** curly

 3. Latin **umor,** a liquid

Can You Spell

advice	agony	climax	loose
advise	camera	humor	lose

E   Take the Second Spelling Test

Review and Evaluation

A **Review the List Words**

Spelling Tip	Learning to recognize Latin and Greek bases can help you in spelling words like **traction** and **hemisphere**.

1. Write the words from the list at the right that have the following Latin and Greek bases.

  a. Latin **ven**   d. Latin **mit**   g. Latin **scrib**

  b. Latin **nom**   e. Latin **vis**   h. Greek **bio**

  c. Latin **audi**   f. Latin **pos**   i. Greek **poli**

Spelling Tip	Learning to recognize the prefixes **de–** and **dis–** can help you in spelling the first syllable in words like **despise** and **discuss**.

2. Write the list words that have the following respellings. Underline the prefix **de–** or **dis–** in each word.

  a. /di sper'/   d. /di prīv'/

  b. /dis pėrs'/   e. /di struk' shən/

  c. /di sī' siv/   f. /dis' trə byü' shən/

Spelling Tip	The best way to learn words with irregular spellings is to use the study steps on page 5. plateau kindergarten gymnasium

3. Write the list words represented by the dictionary respellings below. Check with the words at the right if you need help with any spellings.

  a. /ok' sə jən/   d. /am' ə chər/

  b. /bak tir' ē ə/   e. /ag' rə kul' chər/

  c. /sour' krout'/   f. /ôk' wərd/

agriculture
amateur
antibiotic
audition
awkward
bacteria
decisive
deprive
despair
destruction
disperse
distribution
intervention
nominate
oxygen
policy
remittance
sauerkraut
transcribe
transpose
visualize

More List Words to Review

1. Write the list words that have the following respellings. Underline the letters that spell an unstressed vowel sound represented by /ə/. Check with the words at the right if you need help with any spellings.

a. /em′ ər əld/   c. /kə kün′/

b. /jē ol′ ə jē/   d. /kus′ tə dē/

2. Write the list words that have the following respellings. Underline all the letters that spell the /i/ sound. Check with the words at the right if you need help with any spellings.

a. /sinj/   c. /pir′ ə mid/

b. /an′ tə nimz/   d. /sin′ ə nimz/

3. Write the list words that have these respellings. Underline the letters that spell the /f/ sound in each word.

a. /hem′ ə sfir/   c. /bī og′ rə fē/

b. /am fib′ ē ən/   d. /strat′ ə sfir/

4. Write **smother** and **sponge.** Underline the letter that spells the /u/ sound in each word.

5. Write **plateau** and **oath.** Underline the letters that spell the /ō/ sound in each word.

6. Write **spaghetti** and **disguise.** Underline the letter that follows **g** in each word.

7. Write **aquarium, colloquial, eloquent,** and **loquacious.** Underline the letters that spell /kw/ in each word.

amphibian
antonyms
aquarium
biography
cocoon
colloquial
custody
disguise
eloquent
emerald
geology
hemisphere
loquacious
oath
plateau
pyramid
singe
smother
spaghetti
sponge
stratosphere
synonyms

Take the First Review Test

Copy the following sentences. Complete each sentence by writing the correct one of the two words given in parentheses. Check with the Speller Dictionary if you need help with any meanings.

1. (plain, plane) The message on the note was — .

2. (council, counsel) The — voted to accept the plan.

3. (fir, fur) We planted a — tree in our backyard.

4. (advice, advise) Dave asked for my — .

5. (boy, buoy) The flashing — signaled danger.

6. (cents, sense) His answer makes no — .

7. (loose, lose) How did you — the theater tickets?

8. (alley, ally) My — came to my defense.

9. (decent, descent) The skier made a smooth — .

10. (cereal, serial) I watch the TV — every weekday.

11. (straight, strait) The ship passed slowly through the — .

12. (aboard, abroad) Julie has lived — for two years.

Can You Spell These Language Words

alphabet	hyphen	parentheses
apostrophe	italics	phoneme
asterisk	metaphor	simile
diphthong	morpheme	syllable
homophone	paragraph	symbol

    Take the Second Review Test

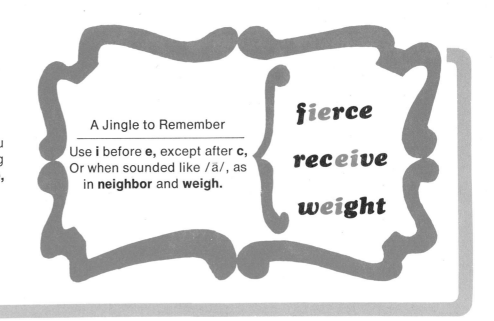

How can the jingle help you remember the **ie–ei** spelling in words like **fierce, receive,** and **weight?**

A Jingle to Remember

Use **i** before **e,** except after **c,**
Or when sounded like /ā/, as in **neighbor** and **weigh.**

fierce

receive

weight

A The ie–ei Problem

All the list words at the right contain either **ie** or **ei.** The jingle won't help you remember the **ie–ei** spelling in all these words, but it will help you with most of them. Say the list words. Decide which words follow the regular pattern for using **ie** and **ei** according to the jingle and which words do not.

1. Write the list words in which **i** comes before **e** in keeping with the jingle.

2. Write the list words in which **ei** follows **c.**

3. Write the list words in which **ei** spells the /ā/ sound.

4. Write the list words that do not follow the jingle.

achieve
apiece
believable
ceiling
conceit
diesel
fierce
fiery
frontier
neighborhood

rein
relieve
review
seize
shriek
weird
wield
wiener
windshield
yield

B   Check the Spelling

1. Write the list words represented by the dictionary re-spellings below. Underline the letters that spell the vowel sound represented by /ē/ in each word.

a. /wē′ nər/   e. /sē′ ling/

b. /shrēk/   f. /ə pēs′/

c. /ə chēv′/   g. /yēld/

d. /wēld/   h. /kən sēt′/

a

2. Write the list words that begin with the prefix **re–**.

3. Write **believable** and **diesel.** Underline the letters that spell the /əl/ ending in each word.

Check the Meaning

1. Each picture at the right is a clue to one of the list words. Which list word goes with picture **a**? With picture **b**? Write the words.

b

2. Write the list word that is a synonym for each of the word pairs below. Use the Speller Dictionary if you need help with any of the meanings.

a. employ, use   c. vicinity, community

b. savage, violent   d. flaming, hot

3. Write the list word that is an antonym for each of the following word pairs. Use the Speller Dictionary if you need help.

a. release, free   c. common, usual

b. modesty, humility   d. fail, miss

Can You Spell   piece   receive   reign

C   Take the First Spelling Test

D   Word Challenge

1. The prefix **uni–** means "one," **bi–** means "two," and **tri–** means "three." Copy the following definitions. See if you can complete each one with a number word.

   a. A **unicycle** is a cycle with — wheel.

   b. A **bicycle** is a cycle with — wheels.

   c. A **tricycle** is a cycle with — wheels.

   d. A **unicorn** is an imaginary animal with — horn.

2. Pictures **a** and **b** show two planes that are more than fifty years old. One plane is called a **biplane,** and the other is called a **triplane.** Which plane do you think appears in picture **a?** In picture **b?** Write the names of the planes.

a
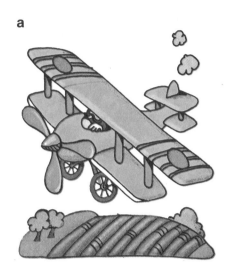

Word Lore

English contains a small number of words that began as trademarks but have since become common, everyday words. The word **escalator** is a typical example. When the first moving staircases appeared, they went under the trademark **Escalator.** Today most people call any moving staircase an **escalator,** no matter what the brand name.

The definitions for three words that were once trademarks but are now common, everyday words are given below. Write the word that goes with each definition. Choose the words from the list in the box.

   1. a medicine

   2. a type of cloth

   3. a machine for copying

> nylon
>
> mimeograph
>
> aspirin

b

Can You Spell

biplane	mimeograph	tricycle	unicorn
escalator	nylon	triplane	unicycle

E   Take the Second Spelling Test

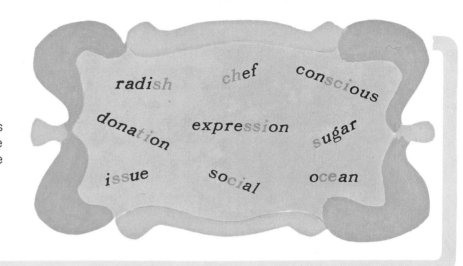

radish chef conscious

donation expression sugar

issue social ocean

? How many different spellings for the /sh/ sound do these words illustrate? What are they?

A Spelling the /sh/ Sound

All the list words at the right contain the /sh/ sound. Say the words, and check the spelling of the /sh/ sound in each word.

1. Write the list words in which the /sh/ sound is spelled with **sh.**

2. Write the list words in which the /sh/ sound is spelled with **ti.**

3. Write the list words in which the /sh/ sound is spelled with **ci.**

4. Write the list words in which the /sh/ sound is spelled with **ss.**

5. Write the list words in which the /sh/ sound is spelled with **ssi.**

additional
ambition
beneficial
cautious
cherish
congressional
especially
establish
facial
graduation

junction
marshal
obligation
physician
pressure
proficient
session
shallow
shrewd
tissue

Check the Spelling

1. Write the list words that have the following respellings. Underline all the letters that spell an unstressed vowel sound represented by /ə/. Check with the pronunciation key on page 115 and the word list at the right if you need any help.

a. /fə zish′ ən/

c. /ob′ lə gā′ shən/

b. /ben′ ə fish′ əl/

d. /e spesh′· ə lē/

2. Write the list words that end with the **al** spelling for /əl/.

Check the Meaning

Write the list words that you could use to replace the words in heavy type below. Use the Speller Dictionary if you need help with any meanings.

1. Let's meet at the **joining place** of these two roads.

2. A **court officer** led the defendant into the courtroom.

3. The snow put too much **force** on the roof.

4. Jennifer has a **clever** plan for making money.

5. Mr. Carlson is a **very careful** driver.

6. I used a **thin cloth** to polish the table.

7. When did you **set up** the rules for your club?

8. The river is **not deep** at this point.

9. An art collector would **treasure** this painting.

10. A **doctor** examined my sprained ankle.

additional
ambition
beneficial
cautious
cherish
congressional
especially
establish
facial
graduation
junction
marshal
obligation
physician
pressure
proficient
session
shallow
shrewd
tissue

Can You Spell   choose   much   sure

C   Take the First Spelling Test

D Word Challenge

Copy the following definitions. See if you can complete each one with a number word. Remember that the prefix **uni–** means "one," **bi–** means "two," and **tri–** means "three."

1. To **unite** means to make —.

2. To **bisect** means to cut into — equal parts.

3. To **trisect** means to cut into — equal parts.

4. A **bilingual** person can speak — languages.

5. A **trilingual** person can speak — languages.

Word Lore

English contains a number of words that have been formed by shortening other words. For example, **margarine** was formed by dropping the beginning of **oleomargarine,** and **lunch** was formed by dropping the ending of **luncheon.** Words like **margarine** and **lunch** are called **clipped words.**

a. chimpanzee

1. See if you can write the clipped forms for the words shown with pictures **a** and **b** at the right.

2. Copy the second sentence in each pair of sentences below. See if you can complete the sentence by writing the clipped forms for the words in heavy type.

a. The **professional** players had a lot of **pepper.**

The — players had a lot of —.

b. A **telephone** was the actor's only **property.**

A — was the actor's only —.

Can You Spell

bilingual	chimpanzee	stereophonic	trisect
bisect	margarine	trilingual	unite

E Take the Second Spelling Test

b. stereophonic

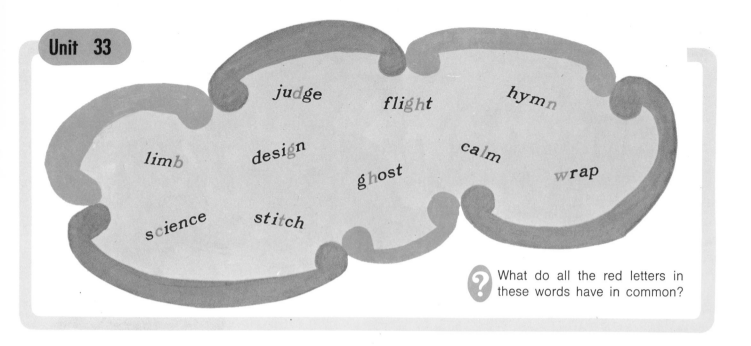

Unit 33

judge flight hymn

limb design calm

ghost wrap

science stitch

What do all the red letters in these words have in common?

Irregular Spellings

1. All the list words at the right contain one or more silent consonants. Say the list words one by one. Note the consonant letters that do not stand for sounds.

2. Write the list words that contain the following silent consonants.

a. The letter **b**

b. The letter **c**

c. The letter **d**

d. The letter **g**

e. The letters **gh**

f. The letter **h**

g. The letter **l**

h. The letter **n**

i. The letter **t**

j. The letter **w**

adjective
almond
assign
autumn
badge
budget
column
doubtful
exhibit
gnaw

muscle
pitcher
plumber
rhyme
scientific
straighten
stretch
thistle
wrench
yolk

Check the Spelling

Write the list words that are related to the following words.

1. columnist
2. muscular
3. assignation
4. exhibition
5. autumnal
6. scientifically
7. adjectival
8. budgetary

Check the Meaning

1. When words are confused, a sentence sometimes has a ridiculous meaning. Copy sentences **a** and **b** under the pictures at the right. Replace each word in heavy type with a list word that makes sense.

2. Write the list word that matches each clue below.

a. You might find this in a bag of mixed nuts.

b. He's a pro when it comes to fixing a leaky faucet.

c. **Dine, sign, shine,** and **vine** are words that do this.

d. Break it, and the egg goes from fried to scrambled.

e. This could be a real pain underfoot.

f. The sheriff wears one, and so does the deputy.

g. A tree might fall when a beaver does this.

h. Make one today, and save money tomorrow.

i. Look for this in a box of tools.

Can You Spell   half   hour   know

C   **Take the First Spelling Test**

a. He poured tea from the **picture.**

b. She got up to **sketch** her legs.

D Word Challenge

1. See if you can write answers to the following questions. Hint: The prefix **tri–** means "three," **quad–** means "four," and **quin–** means "five."

  a. How many singers are there in a **trio**?

  b. How many singers are there in a **quartet**?

  c. How many singers are there in a **quintet**?

  d. How many angles does a **triangle** have?

  e. How many sides does a **quadrilateral** have?

2. One picture at the right could be labeled **quadruplets**, and the other could be labeled **quintuplets**. Which word goes with picture **a**? With picture **b**? Write the words.

a

Word Lore

English contains a number of words that have been formed by combining the spelling and meaning of other words. The word **broast,** for example, combines the spelling and meaning of **broil** and **roast.** The word **brunch** combines the spelling and meaning of **breakfast** and **lunch.** Words like **broast** and **brunch** are called **blends.**

b

See if you can write the blends that have been formed by combining the spelling and meaning of the words below.

  1. motor + hotel
  2. smoke + fog
  3. twist + whirl

  4. flutter + hurry
  5. splash + spatter
  6. squirm + wriggle

Can You Spell

flurry	quadruplets	quintet	splatter
quadrilateral	quartet	quintuplets	squiggle

E Take the Second Spelling Test

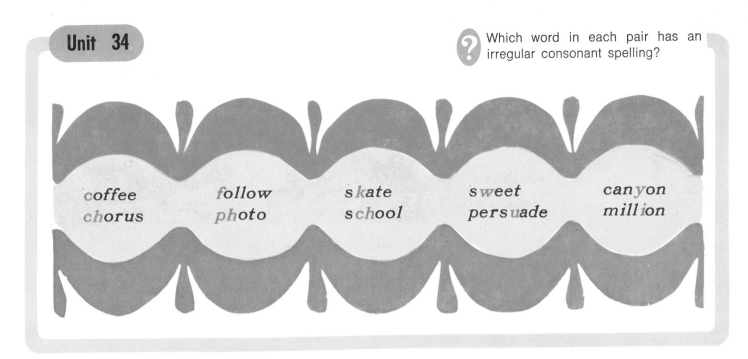

? Which word in each pair has an irregular consonant spelling?

coffee
chorus

follow
photo

skate
school

sweet
persuade

canyon
million

 A More Irregular Spellings

Each list word at the right contains an irregular consonant spelling. Say the words, and see if you can tell what the irregular spellings are.

1. Write the list words that contain the /k/ sound spelled with **ch.**

2. Write the list words that contain the /y/ sound spelled with **i.**

3. Write the list words that contain the /f/ sound spelled with **ph.**

4. Write the list words that contain the /w/ sound spelled with **u.**

5. Write the list words that contain the /k/ sound spelled with **qu** or **que.**

anchor
anguish
character
chrome
civilian
conquer
extinguish
genial
genius
mechanic

orchestra
orphan
penguin
persuade
photography
phrase
scholar
technical
unique
valiant

B   **Check the Spelling**

1. Write the list words that have the following respellings. Underline all the letters that spell an unstressed vowel sound represented by /ə/.

       a. /fə tog′ rə fē/   c. /kar′ ik tər/

       b. /ôr′ kə strə/   d. /sə vil′ yən/

2. Write **anchor** and **scholar.** Underline the letters that spell the /ər/ ending in each word.

3. Write **anguish** and **penguin.** Underline the letter that spells the /w/ sound in each word.

4. Write **unique** and **conquer.** Underline the letters that spell the /k/ sound in each word.

Check the Meaning

1. Write the list words you could use to replace the words in heavy type in each of the following sentences. Use the Speller Dictionary if you need help with any meanings.

a. The auto **repairman** polished the **metal** on the car.

b. They made a **courageous** effort to **put out** the fire.

2. Write the list words that go with the following pairs of synonyms.

       a. influence, convince   d. fasten, secure

       b. cheerful, kind   e. unequaled, different

       c. torment, pain   f. overcome, overpower

Can You Spell   cough   fourth   trouble

C   **Take the First Spelling Test**

anchor
anguish
character
chrome
civilian
conquer
extinguish
genial
genius
mechanic
orchestra
orphan
penguin
persuade
photography
phrase
scholar
technical
unique
valiant

Word Challenge

1. Each of the following words names a period of years.

   century   decade   millennium

See if you can write the word that answers each of the following questions. Hint: The prefix **dec–** means "ten," **cent–** means "one hundred," and **mill–** means "one thousand."

   a. What word names a period of 10 years?

   b. What word names a period of 100 years?

   c. What word names a period of 1000 years?

2. Each of the following words names a measure of length.

   decimeter   millimeter   centimeter

See if you can write the word that answers each of the following questions.

   a. What word names 1/10 of a meter?

   b. What word names 1/100 of a meter?

   c. What word names 1/1000 of a meter?

1. Earl of Sandwich

Word Lore

English contains a small number of words that originally came from the names of people. The **saxophone,** for example, was named after Adolphe Sax, the man who invented this musical instrument around 1840. Other words that came from the names of people include **silhouette, diesel, zinnia, poinsettia,** and **guppy.**

See if you can write the English words that came from the names of the people shown at the right.

Can You Spell

centimeter   decimeter   millimeter   saxophone
century   millennium   poinsettia   silhouette

E   Take the Second Spelling Test

2. General A. E. Burnside

Unit 35

> Two **a**'s, two **r**'s, two **m**'s, and a **g**.
> Put them together, and what do you see?

What word can you think of to answer the riddle in the picture below?

A   Troublesome Words

1. Most people have a group of words that they never seem to spell correctly. The word **grammar** is of this type. One way of mastering such a word is to think of a memory clue that will help you remember the spelling. For example, if you have trouble remembering the **−ar** ending in **grammar**, think of the riddle in the picture above.

2. Observe how the following memory clues can help in learning to spell other list words besides **grammar.**

a. **bargain:** Bar + gain spells bargain.

b. **business:** I am in business for myself.

c. **capital:** A capital is a large letter.

d. **dilemma:** Emma is in a dilemma.

e. **principal:** A principal is a pal.

f. **vinegar:** Vine + gar spells vinegar.

argument
bargain
business
capital
cooperate
dessert
dilemma
engineer
exceed
grammar

literature
parallel
principal
proceed
professor
siege
succeed
treason
villain
vinegar

108

Check the Spelling

1. Write the list words that have the following respellings. Underline the double consonant in each word.

a

a. /biz′ nis/   e. /vil′ ən/

b. /par′ ə lel/   f. /də lem′ ə/

c. /di zėrt′/   g. /prə fes′ ər/

d. /sək sēd′/   h. /gram′ ər/

2. Write the list words that end with **ceed.** Remember
that these are the only English words that end with this
spelling.

3. Write the list words that end with **−ar.**

b

4. Write **siege** and **treason.** Underline the letters that
spell the /ē/ sound in each word.

Check the Meaning

1. Pictures **a, b,** and **c** at the right are clues to three list
words. See if you can find and write the words.

2. Copy the following sentences. Complete each one with
two list words. Use the Speller Dictionary if you need help
with any meanings.

c

a. Dr. Bruner was a — of English —.

b. The — ended when the two boys began to —.

c. The — signaled the train to — on its journey.

d. A huge amount of — was invested in the new —.

Can You Spell   capitol   desert   principle

C   **Take the First Spelling Test**

Word Challenge

Study the examples below to discover why the word **disobey** has one **s** and the word **dissolve** has two.

> dis + obey → disobey
> dis + solve → dissolve

Now see if you can apply the same pattern in combining the following words and prefixes. Write the words.

1. dis + appoint
2. un + afraid
3. mis + understood
4. dis + service
5. un + necessary
6. mis + spell

Word Lore

English contains a number of words that originally came from the names of places. **Cantaloupe** (named after Cantalupo, Italy) and **tangerine** (named after Tangier, Morocco) are two examples. Others are listed below.

cologne   italics   suede
duffel bag   limerick   tuxedo

1. See if you can write the words that came from these place names.

a. Cologne, Germany
b. Tuxedo Park, New York
c. Limerick, Ireland
d. Duffel, Belgium

2. See if you can write the words that came from the place names at the right.

Can You Spell

cantaloupe   disappoint   misunderstood   tangerine
cologne   misspell   suede   unnecessary

Take the Second Spelling Test

a. Italy

b. Sweden

Review and Evaluation

A

Review the List Words

Spelling Tip	The following jingle will help you spell most of the **ie–ei** words that you know.
	Use **i** before **e**,
	except after **c**,
	Or when sounded like /ā/,
	as in **neighbor** and **weigh**.

1. Write the following list words correctly. Add **ie** or **ei** according to the jingle.

a. conc–t   c. ach–ve   e. c–ling

b. r–n   d. f–ry   f. front–r

Spelling Tip	The best way to learn words with irregular spellings is to use the study helps on page 5.

2. Write the list words represented by the dictionary respellings below. Check with the words at the right if you need help.

a. /ang′ gwish/   e. /strech/

b. /tish′ ü/   f. /ek sting′ gwish/

c. /nô/   g. /rench/

d. /aj′ ik tiv/   h. /jē′ nyəs/

Spelling Tip	Memory clues like "A principal is a pal" can often be of help in learning to spell troublesome words.

3. Write the list words represented by the following respellings. Try to think of memory clues that will help you with the spellings.

a. /sək sēd′/   c. /vil′ ən/   e. /də lem′ ə/

b. /par′ ə lel/   d. /di zėrt′/   f. /biz′ nis/

achieve
adjective
anguish
business
ceiling
conceit
dessert
dilemma
extinguish
fiery
frontier
genius
gnaw
parallel
rein
stretch
succeed
tissue
villain
wrench

More List Words to Review

1. Write the list words that have the following respellings. Underline all the letters that spell an unstressed vowel sound represented by /ə/. Check with the words at the right if you need help with any spellings.

a. /jungk′ shən/

b. /kô′ shəs/

c. /sī′ ən tif′ ik/

d. /kən gresh′ ə nəl/

e. /kar′ ik tər/

f. /fə tog′ rə fē/

g. /lit′ ər ə chur/

h. /är′ gyə mənt/

argument
cautious
character
congressional
diesel
fierce
gnaw
junction
literature
photography
physician
rhyme
scientific
seize
shrewd
siege
technical
thistle
unique
weird

2. Write the list words that name the objects in pictures **a** and **b.** Underline the letters that spell the /əl/ ending in each word.

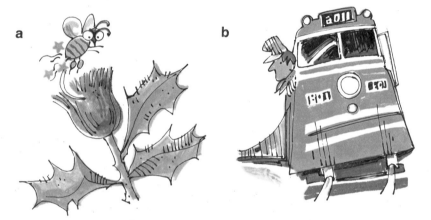

a

b

3. Write **technical** and **unique.** Underline all the letters that spell the /k/ sound in the words.

4. Write **physician** and **rhyme.** Notice the sound that the **y** has in each word.

5. Write **seize** and **siege.** Underline the letters that spell the /ē/ sound in each word.

6. Write **fierce** and **weird.** Underline the letters that spell the vowel sound before the **r** in each word.

7. Write **gnaw** and **shrewd.** Underline the two letters that spell the vowel sound in each word.

C

Take the First Review Test

D   Review the Challenging Words

Prefix	Meaning
uni–	one
bi–	two
tri–	three
quad–	four
quin–	five
dec–	ten
cent–	one hundred
mill–	one thousand

1. Copy each definition below. See if you can complete the definitions with number words. Check with the chart at the right if you have a question about the meaning of any number prefixes.

a. A **unicorn** is an imaginary animal with — horn.

b. A **unicycle** is a cycle with — wheel.

c. A **bilingual** person can speak — languages.

d. A **trilingual** person can speak — languages.

e. A **quartet** is a singing group with — members.

f. A **century** is a period of — years.

g. A **millennium** is a period of — years.

h. A **decimeter** is — of a meter.

i. A **centimeter** is — of a meter.

j. A **millimeter** is — of a meter.

2. See what words you can write by combining the following words and prefixes. Check with the examples at the right if you need help in deciding whether a word should have a double consonant or not.

dis + obey → disobey

dis + solve → dissolve

a. dis + appoint   c. mis + spell

b. mis + understood   d. un + necessary

Can You Spell These Math Words

bisector   exponent   quotient
circumference   inequality   subtraction
congruent   intersection   transversal
decagon   interval   triangular
distributive   quadrant   trigonometry

E   Take the Second Review Test

Speller Dictionary

The Pronunciation Key is used by permission of the publishers of the Thorndike-Barnhart Intermediate Dictionary, Copyright © 1971 by Scott, Foresman and Company, Glenview, Ill.

A

a board /ə bôrd′/ *prep.* In, on, or into a train, airplane, boat, or other vehicle. *The passengers will start coming* **aboard** *this liner in a few minutes.* —*adv.* In, on, or into a vehicle.

a broad /ə brôd′/ *adv.* In a foreign country. *My brother has been studying* **abroad** *for two years.*

ab so lute /ab′ sə lüt/ *adj.* **1.** Complete; entire. *The driver was in* **absolute** *control of the car.* **2.** Positive; certain.

ab sorb /ab sôrb′/ *v.* To take in or soak up. *The sponge* **absorbed** *almost all of the water.*

ac cent /ak′ sent/ *n.* **1.** The stress or emphasis given to a syllable or to a note in music. *In the word* actor *the* **accent** *is on the first syllable.* **2.** A mark showing the syllable to be emphasized.

ac ces sor y /ak ses′ ər ē *or* ak ses′ rē/ *n., pl.* ACCESSORIES. That which is added to make something more attractive or convenient. *The scarf was the perfect* **accessory** *Beth needed to complete her outfit.*

ac ci den tal ly /ak′ sə den′ təl ē *or* ak′ sə dent′-lē/ *adv.* By accident; by chance.

ac com plish /ə kom′ plish/ *v.* To do successfully; to complete. *I* **accomplished** *all I had planned to do.*

ac cur ate /ak′ yər it/ *adj.* Exactly correct, usually as the result of painstaking work.

ac cuse /ə kyüz′/ *v.,* ACCUSED, ACCUSING. **1.** To blame or find fault with. *Drive more slowly, or the officer will* **accuse** *you of speeding.* **2.** To charge with a crime.

a chieve /ə chēv′/ *v.,* ACHIEVED, ACHIEVING. To gain; to reach; to accomplish. *What do you expect to* **achieve** *by such action?*

ac tion /ak′ shən/ *n.* **1.** The act of doing something. *Her quick* **action** *prevented an accident.* **2.** Battle.

ac tiv i ty /ak tiv′ ə tē/ *n., pl.* ACTIVITIES. **1.** The state or quality of being in action or motion. *She is a typical athlete, and she enjoys physical* **activity.** **2.** An event.

ac tor /ak′ tər/ *n.* A person who performs in a stage, motion-picture, television, or radio play. *My cousin wants to become an* **actor.**

ac tu al /ak′ chü əl/ *adj.* Real; existing in fact; not imaginary.

a dapt /ə dapt′/ *v.* To adjust or correct; to make suitable or fitting. *The animal* **adapted** *itself to changes in climate.*

ad di tion al /ə dish′ ə nəl/ *adj.* More than the original amount. *There are* **additional** *paper napkins in the cupboard in case we need them.*

ad jec tive /aj′ ik tiv/ *n.* A word used to modify a noun or a pronoun.

ad mir a ble /ad′ mər ə bəl/ *adj.* **1.** That which is worth admiring. *Your tact in handling the matter is* **admirable.** **2.** Outstanding; excellent.

ad mire /ad mīr′/ *v.,* ADMIRED, ADMIRING. To feel high esteem for or to show keen approval of. *I* **admire** *the dancer's rhythm and grace.*

ad mis sion /ad mish′ ən/ *n.* **1.** The act of allowing entrance. **Admission** *to the party was by invitation only.* **2.** The price paid to be allowed to enter.

ad van ta geous /ad′ vən tā′ jəs/ *adj.* Favorable; profitable. *Now is an* **advantageous** *time to sell your property.*

ad verb /ad′ verb′/ *n.* A word used to modify a verb, an adjective, or another adverb.

ad ver tise ment /ad′ vər tīz′ mənt *or* ad ver′- tis mənt/ *n.* An announcement or a notice in a magazine, in a newspaper, on television, etc.

ad vice /ad vīs′/ *n.* Instruction; information. *I can give you **advice**, but I can't make you follow it.*

ad vise /ad vīz′/ *v.,* ADVISED, ADVISING. To give advice to. *What do you **advise** me to do, Mr. Clark?*

a gen cy /ā′ jən sē/ *n., pl.* AGENCIES. The office of an agent or business representative.

ag ri cul ture /ag′ rə kul′ chər/ *n.* Farming. *Which European countries are best suited for **agriculture?*** [Latin *agricultura*]

a lert /ə lert′/ *adj.* Watchful; ready to act instantly. *A good watchdog is **alert**.* [Italian *all'erta,* on the watchtower]

al ler gy /al′ ər jē/ *n., pl.* ALLERGIES. Sensitiveness to certain things. *The boy had an **allergy** to milk and other dairy products.*

al ley /al′ ē/ *n., pl.* ALLEYS. **1.** A narrow passageway between buildings in a city or a town. *The **alley** behind our house is paved.* **2.** A place for playing certain kinds of games, such as bowling.

al lot ment /ə lot′ mənt/ *n.* That which has been divided into portions or shares. *This month your **allotment** comes to 2,000 cases of pressed beef.*

al low ance /ə lou′ əns/ *n.* A certain amount of money given periodically.

all read y /ôl′ red′ ē/ All prepared. *We are **all ready** now.*

al ly¹ /al′ ī *or* ə lī′/ *n., pl.* ALLIES. One joined to another, usually by a formal agreement such as a treaty; an associate. *The United States and England were **allies** during World War II.*

al ly² /ə lī′/ *v.,* ALLIED, ALLYING. To unite for some special purpose. *One country may*

ally itself with another for defense against a common enemy.

al mond /äm′ ənd *or* am′ ənd/ *n.* A nut; the seed of a tropical fruit.

al read y /ôl red′ ē/ *adv.* By this time. *The visitors have **already** arrived.*

al ter a tion /ôl′ tə rā′ shən/ *n.* The act of changing certain parts or details. *The **alteration** of Jane's dress will not require much time.*

al ter na tion /ôl′ tər nā′ shən/ *n.* An arrangement by turns in which first one thing occurs and then the other. *The **alternation** of black and gold uniforms gave the band a striking appearance.*

a lu mi num /ə lü′ mə nəm/ *n.* A silver-white, very lightweight metal that does not rust; it is used to make cooking pots and pans, automobile bodies, and airplane parts where lightness is desired.

am a teur /am′ ə chər *or* am′ ə tər/ *n.* **1.** A person who writes, paints, etc., for pleasure, not money. *My father is an **amateur** photographer.* **2.** An adult who participates in organized sports for pleasure, not money. [French *amateur*]

am bi tion /am bish′ ən/ *n.* **1.** A great desire to gain or become some definite thing. *Frank's **ambition** drove him to work harder and harder.* **2.** The goal which one desires most.

am phib i an /am fib′ ē ən/ *n.* **1.** An animal or plant able to live both on land and in water. *A salamander is an **amphibian**.* **2.** An airplane designed to rise from and light on either land or water. —*adj.* Capable of living or operating on land or water.

am pli fy /am′ plə fī/ *v.,* AMPLIFIED, AMPLIFYING. **1.** To make larger, louder, stronger, etc. *A loudspeaker is a device used to **amplify** sound.* **2.** To expand.

an chor /ang′ kər/ *v.* To fix or fasten firmly; to

hat, āge, fär; let, ēqual, term; it, īce; hot, ōpen, ôrder; oil, out; cup, put, rüle; ch, child; ng, long; sh, she; th, thin; ᴛн, then; zh, measure; ə represents *a* in about, *e* in taken, *i* in pencil, *o* in lemon, *u* in circus.

make secure in one place. *The girls anchored the tent at several points.—n.* **1.** A heavy piece of iron which, when attached to a cable, is used to hold a boat in place. **2.** Anything that holds something in one position.

an gle /ang′ gəl/ *n.* A geometric figure formed by the intersection of two straight lines. *Draw a triangle having one right angle.*

an guish /ang′ gwish/ *n.* Torment; pain; distress. *The mother of the lost child was sick with anguish.*

an ni ver sa ry /an′ ə vėr′ sər ē *or* an′ ə vėrs′ rē/ *n., pl.* ANNIVERSARIES. **1.** The yearly return of the day on which an event happened. *Mr. and Mrs. Mitchell have celebrated their fiftieth wedding anniversary.* **2.** A celebration of the yearly return of a date.

an ti bi ot ic /an′ ti bī ot′ ik/ *n.* A chemical substance such as penicillin used for fighting disease-causing bacteria, viruses, etc.

an to nym /an′ tə nim/ *n.* A word that means the opposite of another word. *Hope and despair are antonyms.*

a piece /ə pēs′/ *adv.* To or for each one. *The candy canes cost three cents apiece.*

ap o gee /ap′ ə jē/ *n.* The point in the orbit of a spacecraft when the spacecraft is farthest from the earth. *An orbiting spacecraft reaches its slowest speed at apogee.*

ap par ent /ə par′ ənt *or* ə per′ ənt/ *adj.* Obvious; easily seen; distinct; plain.

ap pear ance /ə pir′ ens/ *n.* **1.** The act of coming before the public. *He is soon to make an appearance on television.* **2.** The outward look of a person or object.

ap ple sauce /ap′ əl sôs′/ *n.* A sauce made from apples. *Do you like applesauce?*

ap pli ca tion /ap′ lə kā′ shən/ *n.* **1.** A written or oral request for employment. *If you are interested in this kind of work, make your application at once.* **2.** The process of putting a material on something, as ointment on a burn. **3.** Putting to use.

ap proach /ə prōch′/ *v.* To come near. *We approached the robin's nest very quietly.—n.* **1.** The act of coming near, either in time or space, as the approach of one's birthday. **2.** The means or way by which one arrives, as the approach to a garage.

a quar i um /ə kwer′ ē əm *or* ə kwar′ ē əm/ *n.* **1.** A pond, tank, or bowl in which living fishes or other water animals and plants are kept. *The cat gazed longingly at the aquarium.* **2.** A building which houses an aquarium. [Latin *aquarius*, of water]

arch er y /är′ chər ē *or* ärch′ rē/ *n.* The art of shooting with bows and arrows.

ar gu ment /är′ gyə mənt/ *n.* A discussion for and against. *The boys were having an argument on the merits of using minnows for fish bait.*

ar ter y /är′ tər ē/ *n., pl.* ARTERIES. **1.** A vessel which carries the blood from the heart through the body. *The blood in an artery is bright red because it contains oxygen.* **2.** A channel of communication.

ar ti cle /är′ tə kəl/ *n.* **1.** A thing; a separate element or part. *Every article of my fishing tackle was in its proper place.* **2.** In writing, a composition that is complete within itself and yet part of a larger publication, such as a magazine or newspaper.

as pir in /as′ pər ən *or* as′ prən/ *n.* A drug used as a remedy for pain or fever.

as sign /ə sīn′/ *v.* **1.** To prescribe or allot. *The teacher assigned work to each pupil.* **2.** To appoint or name definitely.

as sist /ə sist′/ *v.* To help. *He assisted the coach during the game.*

as sume /ə süm′/ *v.,* ASSUMED, ASSUMING. **1.** To take for granted. *He seems to assume that he will be elected.* **2.** To pretend.

as sur ance /ə shùr′ əns/ *n.* **1.** The feeling of being sure or confident. *Faithful daily work gives one assurance in facing an examination.* **2.** A guarantee; a pledge.

as sure /ə shur'/ v., ASSURED, ASSURING. To make sure; to state positively and with confidence. *I assure you that the bill will be paid.*

at tain /ə tān'/ v. To arrive or reach; to gain; to accomplish. *By great effort she attained success in the business world.*

at tend ance /ə ten' dəns/ n. **1.** The act of attending. *His attendance was unexpected.* **2.** The company of persons present.

at tract /ə trakt'/ v. To draw towards or pull towards.

auc tion /ôk' shən/ n. A public sale at which an article is sold to the person who offers to pay the most money for it. *I bought the walnut table at an auction.* — v. To sell at an auction.

au di ence /ô' dē əns/ n. **1.** A group of people who have come together to hear or see. *The audience enjoyed the motion picture.* **2.** A hearing or interview.

au di tion /ô dish' ən/ n. A hearing given to test a speaker or performer. *The young singer tried many times to get an audition with the producer.* — v. To give such a hearing.

au di to ri um /ô' də tôr' ē əm/ n. A large room or hall used for public gatherings; a place for an audience.

au tumn /ô' təm/ n. The season of the year which comes between summer and winter, often called the fall.

awk ward /ôk' wərd/ adj. **1.** Clumsy; lacking skill. *The awkward waiter tripped on my foot.* **2.** Hard to handle; inconvenient. [Scandinavian *ofugr*, facing the wrong way]

B

bach e lor /bach' ə lər *or* bach' lər/ n. **1.** An unmarried man. *He is a bachelor and lives in a small apartment.* **2.** Any person who has earned the first degree granted by a college or university.

bac ter i a /bak tir' ē ə/ n. Microorganisms that are widely distributed in air, water, and soil. *Some bacteria cause disease; others are beneficial.* [Greek *bakterion*, little stick]

badge /baj/ n. An emblem worn to show that one belongs to a certain occupation or organization.

bal lot /bal' ət/ v. To cast a secret vote. *We balloted for a new secretary.* — n. A means of casting a secret vote, especially a piece of paper upon which the candidates' names appear.

band age /ban' dij/ n. A strip of cloth used in binding up wounds or injured parts of the body. *A bandage should be a piece of clean gauze.* — v., BANDAGED, BANDAGING. To wrap or dress a wound.

bar gain /bär' gən/ n. **1.** An agreement to buy or sell something at a certain price. *I found that I'd made a poor bargain.* **2.** That which is bought or sold at a cheap price. — v. To try to get better terms in a transaction.

bar ren /bar' ən/ adj. Unproductive. *The area was so barren that we did not see a single blade of grass on our morning's walk.*

ba sis /bā' sis/ n., pl. BASES /-sēz/. **1.** A foundation; base or main part. *The basis of this story is an actual event.* **2.** A common ground.

bat ter /bat' ər/ n. **1.** One who uses a bat, as in baseball. *The batter hit a long foul ball.* **2.** A thin mixture made by beating flour, eggs, and milk together. — v. To pound or strike repeatedly.

bea con /bē' kən/ n. **1.** A signal light used for guiding aviators or sailors. *The crew members were glad when they saw the beacon.* **2.** The tower or lighthouse where the signal is located.

---

hat, āge, fär; let, ēqual, tėrm; it, īce; hot, ōpen, ôrder; oil, out; cup, put, rüle; ch, child; ng, long; sh, she; th, thin; ŦH, then; zh, measure; ə represents *a* in about, *e* in taken, *i* in pencil, *o* in lemon, *u* in circus.

be liev a ble /bə lē′ və bəl/ *adj.* Capable of being believed.

ben e fi cial /ben′ ə fish′ əl/ *adj.* Helpful or advantageous; favorable. *Penicillin is beneficial in fighting certain bacteria.*

be tray /bi trā′/ *v.* To turn over to an enemy; to be unfaithful to.

bi og ra phy /bī og′ rə fē/ *n., pl.* BIOGRAPHIES. The story of a person's life.

blos som /blos′ əm/ *n.* A flower. *What a lovely apple blossom that is!* —*v.* To bloom. [Old English *blostma*]

bob /bob/ *v.,* BOBBED, BOBBING. To move up and down in short, quick movements. *Pam saw the float bob, and she knew she had a bite.*

bo nus /bō′ nəs/ *n., pl.* BONUSES. Something given in addition to the payment that has been agreed upon. *All persons who had been with the company for a year or more received a bonus.*

boost er ve hi cle /bü′ stər vē′ ə kəl/ *n.* A rocket that is dropped after the extra fuel it carries is burned off. *The booster vehicle fell toward the earth as the rocket's first stage ended and its second stage began.*

bound ar y /boun′ dər ē *or* boun′ drē/ *n., pl.* BOUNDARIES. A limit; a borderline; that which indicates or fixes the limit or extent of a territory. *The boundary of the tennis court should be more distinct.*

boy /boi/ *n.* A young male.

breath /breth/ *n.* Air taken into and out of the lungs by breathing.

breathe /brēth/ *v.,* BREATHED, BREATHING. 1. To draw air into the lungs and let it out. *Running makes me breathe hard.* 2. To pause to take breath.

brick lay er /brik′ lā′ ər/ *n.* One who builds with bricks.

bril liance /bril′ yəns/ *n.* 1. Sparkle; brightness. *We were surprised at the brilliance of the diamond.* 2. Unusual talent or ability.

bron co /brong′ kō/ *n., pl.* BRONCOS. An untamed or only partially tamed horse in the western United States. *The bronco began to buck the minute the cowhand sat on its back.* [Spanish *bronco,* wild]

bruise /brüz/ *n.* An injury that does not break the skin. *A black-and-blue mark on the skin indicates a bruise.* —*v.,* BRUISED, BRUISING. To injure without breaking the skin.

buck a roo /buk′ ə rü′ *or* buk′ ə rü′/ *n., pl.* BUCKAROOS. A cowhand. *The buckaroos herded the ponies into the corral.* [Spanish *vaquero*]

budg et /buj′ it/ *n.* An estimate of the money needed by an individual or an organization within a given period.

buoy /boi *or* bü′ ē/ *n.* A float used for marking the channel in a river or a bay or for marking dangerous spots in rivers, bays, or oceans. *Somehow the buoy had got loose and floated ashore.*

busi ness /biz′ nis/ *n., pl.* BUSINESSES. 1. Any commercial or industrial enterprise. *Mr. Jones is in the grocery business.* 2. A person's occupation or trade.

C

cab i net /kab′ ə nit *or* kab′ nit/ *n.* 1. A piece of furniture equipped with shelves or drawers for storing or displaying articles. *Our medicine cabinet has four shelves.* 2. A group of men or women chosen to act as advisers.

ca boo dle /kə bü′ dəl/ *n. Slang.* A collection of people or things, generally occurring only in the expression "the whole kit and caboodle." *All the furniture—the whole kit and caboodle—was sold at a public auction.*

ca hoots /kə hüts′/ *n. Slang.* Partnership, especially one that is secret. *The two crooks were working in cahoots.*

cal a boose /kal′ ə büs *or* kal′ ə büs′/ *n. Slang.* A prison or jail. *The old calaboose is now a museum showing prison conditions of an earlier day.* [Spanish *calabozo*]

cal en dar /kal′ ən dər/ *n.* **1.** A table or chart of the year, showing the months, weeks, and days. *You will find this tiny calendar convenient to carry in your purse.* **2.** A schedule of events.

can cel /kan′ səl/ *v.* **1.** To strike out with a pen or pencil. *Cancel all the 9's in this column of figures.* **2.** To mark something to show that it is unusable.

can vas /kan′ vəs/ *n., pl.* CANVASES. **1.** A coarse, heavy cloth, usually of hemp or flax. *Tents and sails are made of canvas.* **2.** A picture painted on a canvas.

can vass /kan′ vəs/ *v.* **1.** To solicit or seek for something throughout an area, especially for votes, orders, or work. *We canvassed the community for the Red Cross membership drive.* **2.** To examine or study carefully.

cap i tal /kap′ ə təl/ *n.* **1.** The chief city of a country or state; its seat of government. *Paris is the capital of France.* **2.** A large letter. **3.** The stock or money used in carrying on a business.

cap i tol /kap′ ə təl/ *n.* **1.** A statehouse. *The capitol of our state is visited by hundreds of schoolchildren each year.* **2.** *(with a capital letter)* The building in Washington, D.C., where Congress meets.

ca reer /kə rir′/ *n.* A profession requiring special preparation. *His career as a lawyer was cut short by an automobile accident.* [French *carrière*]

car ni val /kär′ nə vəl/ *n.* A place of amusement providing various means of entertainment.

car ton /kärt′ ən/ *n.* A cardboard box. *I prefer to buy milk in a carton.*

car toon /kär tün′/ *n.* A pictorial sketch, frequently a caricature. *A cartoon of Theodore Roosevelt usually pictures him with heavy-rimmed glasses and an exaggerated grin.*

cat e go ry /kat′ ə gôr′ ē/ *n., pl.* CATEGORIES. A general classification. *I find that most people can be grouped into two categories— those who talk too much and those who talk too little.*

cau tious /kô′ shəs/ *adj.* Very careful; taking no chances.

ce dar /sē′ dər/ *n.* **1.** An evergreen tree, the wood of which is fragrant, reddish, and very durable. *This kind of cedar grows in Japan.* **2.** The wood from the cedar tree. —*adj.* Made of cedar.

ceil ing /sē′ ling/ *n.* **1.** The inside, overhead surface of a room. *Mother expects to have this ceiling papered.* **2.** The top part of anything as viewed from below. **3.** A maximum price or fee; top limit.

cel er y /sel′ ər ē *or* sel′ rē/ *n.* A vegetable, the long stalks of which are the edible part.

cent /sent/ *n.* A penny. *May I borrow ten cents?*

cer e al /sir′ ē əl/ *n.* A grain such as wheat, oats, barley, corn, or rice; also, a breakfast food made from such a grain.

cer tif i cate /sər tif′ ə kit/ *n.* A statement verifying the authenticity of a claim. *I have a certificate showing I attended summer school last year.*

cer ti fy /sėr′ tə fī/ *v.,* CERTIFIED, CERTIFYING. To guarantee to be genuine or of good quality. *The board of health has certified this milk.*

chal leng er /chal′ ən jər/ *n.* One who calls or dares another to engage in a contest. *Our team is the challenger in the debate.*

char ac ter /kar′ ik tər/ *n.* **1.** The sum of personal qualities that make up one's nature.

---

hat, āge, fär; let, ēqual, tėrm; it, īce; hot, ōpen, ôrder; oil, out; cup, pùt, rüle; ch, child; ng, long; sh, she; th, thin; ᵗн, then; zh, measure; ə represents *a* in about, *e* in taken, *i* in pencil, *o* in lemon, *u* in circus.

*One's **character** is influenced by the habits one has formed.* **2.** Excellent moral repute. **3.** A letter, sign, or figure. **4.** A person in a play or story.

cher ish /cher′ ish/ *v.* To treasure or prize; to treat with affection. *I **cherished** the gift as a sign of our friendship.*

chim ney /chim′ nē/ *n.* A smokestack; an upright hollow structure to carry away smoke. *The **chimneys** extend above the roof.*

chrome /krōm/ *n.* A silver-white metal, highly resistant to corrosion. *Tables and chairs often have legs made of **chrome**.*

cir cu lar /sėr′ kyə lər/ *adj.* Round; having the shape of a circle. *There are several **circular** flower beds in the park.—n.* A letter or pamphlet intended for distribution among a number of people.

cir cu late /sėr′ kyə lāt/ *v.*, CIRCULATED, CIRCULATING. **1.** To move around. *Blood is **circulated** through the body by means of arteries and veins.* **2.** To pass from hand to hand.

cir cum stance /sėr′ kəm stans/ *n.* An event or condition that influences another event. *The snowstorm was a **circumstance** which we couldn't change.*

civ il /siv′ əl/ *adj.* **1.** Pertaining to citizens, especially those within a community or state. *One of my **civil** duties is to pay my taxes.* **2.** Pertaining to civic affairs as distinguished from military, naval, or church affairs. **3.** Reasonably courteous.

ci vil ian /sə vil′ yən/ *n.* A person who is not a member of an army or navy.

clas si fy /klas′ ə fī/ *v.*, CLASSIFIED, CLASSIFYING. To arrange in groups. *I need some help in **classifying** these butterflies for my science project.*

cloth /klôth/ *n.*, *pl.* CLOTHS /klôths *or* klôᵺz/. A piece of material. *Do you have any old **cloths** I can use in washing the car?*

clothes /klōz *or* klōᵺz/ *n.* Garments used to cover the body. *I washed **clothes** today.*

coarse ness /kôrs′ nis/ *n.* Roughness. *I was surprised at the **coarseness** of the sand.*

co coon /kə kün′/ *n.* A silky covering in which insects such as moths spend the period in which they change from the pupa to the adult stage. *The apple tree was full of **cocoons**.* [French *cocon*]

col lage /kə läzh′/ *n.* A kind of picture made by pasting parts of magazines, photographs, string, yarn, etc., onto a background. *I made a **collage** from some of my vacation pictures to show highlights of the trip.*

col lege /kol′ ij/ *n.* A school of higher learning which grants degrees.

col lo qui al /kə lō′ kwē əl/ *adj.* Conversational. *You should try not to use **colloquial** expressions in your formal writing.*

co lo ni al /kə lō′ nē əl/ *adj.* **1.** Pertaining to a colony or colonies. *Many European countries held **colonial** possessions before World War II.* **2.** Relating to the thirteen British colonies which later became part of the United States.

col o nist /kol′ ə nist/ *n.* An inhabitant of a colony; one who helps to found a colony.

col o ny /kol′ ə nē/ *n.*, *pl.* COLONIES. **1.** A group of people who have emigrated to another country, but who still remain citizens of their own country. *The Pilgrim **colony** came to America in search of religious freedom.* **2.** The territory or settlement established by such a group of people.

co los sal /kə los′ əl/ *adj.* Gigantic; enormous; huge. *The building of the Suez Canal was a **colossal** undertaking.*

col umn /kol′ əm/ *n.* **1.** A pillar or structure used to support or adorn a building. *Greek architects made prominent use of the **column**.* **2.** A body of troops following one another in single file. **3.** A perpendicular line of figures in a book or other publication. **4.** A vertical section of a newspaper devoted to treatment of a certain kind of news.

com bi na tion /kom′ bə nā′ shən/ *n.* The state of being united.

com merce /kom′ ərs/ *n.* The buying and selling of goods in large amounts; trade. *Any large city is a center of **commerce**.*

com mit ment /kə mit′ mənt/ *n.* A promise to fulfill certain agreements. *The contractor made a **commitment** to finish the work by June 1.*

com mu ni ty /kə myü′ nə tē/ *n., pl.* COMMUNI-TIES. A group of people living in the same district or having the same interests.

com pen sa tion /kom′ pən sā′ shən/ *n.* **1.** Anything given to make up for something else. *There is no **compensation** for the sacrifices my parents have made for me.* **2.** Pay or amends for loss sustained.

com plaint /kəm plānt′/ *n.* The act of expressing resentment, pain, or grief. *The manager listened patiently to the customer's **complaint** about the scuffed shoes.*

com pu ta tion /kom′ pyə tā′ shən/ *n.* The process of reckoning; finding an arithmetical result. *We made several mistakes in our **computation**.*

con ceal /kən sēl′/ *v.* To keep from sight; to hide. *The thief kept the gun well **concealed**.*

con ceit /kən sēt′/ *n.* Vanity; excessive self-satisfaction; pride. *His **conceit** was shown in the way he strutted down the street.*

con clu sion /kən klü′ zhən/ *n.* **1.** The end. *At the **conclusion** of the lecture, everyone applauded.* **2.** A final decision reached by reasoning.

con fi dence /kon′ fə dəns/ *n.* Trust or certainty. *We have little **confidence** in him.*

con fir ma tion /kon′ fər mā′ shən/ *n.* Proof; verification. *I have just received **confirmation** that Mr. Jensen's explanation is true.*

con flict[1] /kon′ flikt/ *n.* A fight; a struggle between opposing forces. *The **conflict** between the American colonists and England resulted eventually in independence.*

con flict[2] /kən flikt′/ *v.* To struggle; to be in opposition. *Does the time of the meeting **conflict** with your schedule?*

con fu sion /kən fyü′ zhən/ *n.* The state or condition of being bewildered or mistaken.

con gres sion al /kən gresh′ ə nəl/ *adj.* Belonging or pertaining to a congress. *On this side of the building are a number of **congressional** offices.*

con nip tion /kə nip′ shən/ *n. Slang.* A fit of excitement or rage. *The cleaning person had a **conniption** when we got our muddy footprints on the clean floor.*

con quer /kong′ kər/ *v.* To overcome or subdue. *He **conquered** the bad habit with sheer determination.*

con ser va tion /kon′ sər vā′ shən/ *n.* The preservation of anything, especially natural resources. *We are all interested in the **conservation** of our forests.*

con sid er a tion /kən sid′ ə rā′ shən/ *n.* **1.** Attention. *Has Mrs. Brown given any **consideration** to our proposal?* **2.** Thoughtfulness.

con sul /kon′ səl/ *n.* A person appointed by a government to live in another country in order to look after the first country's interests, especially commercial interests. *I delivered the message to the Italian **consul** in New York City.*

con ti nent /kon′ tə nənt/ *n.* Any one of the seven great land masses of the globe. *The **continent** of North America and the **continent** of South America are connected by the Isthmus of Panama.*

con tin u al ly /kən tin′ yü ə lē *or* kən tin′-yü lē/ *adv.* **1.** Without stopping; unceasing. *Rain fell **continually** for two days and nights.* **2.** Occurring in rapid succession over a period of time.

---

hat, āge, fär; let, ēqual, tėrm; it, īce; hot, ōpen, ȯrder; oil, out; cup, pu̇t, rüle; ch, child; ng, long; sh, she; th, thin; ₮H, then; zh, measure; ə represents *a* in about, *e* in taken, *i* in pencil, *o* in lemon, *u* in circus.

con tin u a tion /kən tin′ yü ā′ shən/ *n.* The act of starting again after having stopped for a while.

con tra ry /kon′ trer ē/ *adj.* Opposed in purpose; completely counter. *Contrary to their parents' wishes, they left high school before graduating.* —*n.* The opposite.

con vene /kən vēn′/ *v.,* CONVENED, CONVENING. 1. To assemble. *The convention will convene at nine o'clock tomorrow morning.* 2. To call together.

con vey ance /kən vā′ əns/ *n.* Any kind of vehicle. *Through the ages people have used many types of conveyances, from sledges dragged by oxen to jets and rockets.*

co op e rate /kō op′ ə rāt′/ *v.,* COOPERATED, COOPERATING. To work in harmony with another or others.

cop y right /kop′ ē rīt′/ *n.* A patent given by the government protecting any written work from being reproduced without the consent of the author. *Andrew has obtained a copyright for the play.* —*v.* To obtain a copyright for.

cor por al /kôr′ pər əl *or* kôr′ prəl/ *n.* The lowest-ranking noncommissioned army officer. *Ted has just been made a corporal.*

cos tume /kos′ tüm *or* kos′ tyüm/ *n.* Clothing, especially a fancy dress for some special occasion.

coun cil /koun′ səl/ *n.* 1. An assembly of people gathered to deliberate and act in an advisory capacity. *A council of parents and teachers is studying school-lunch problems.* 2. A group of people elected or appointed to manage the affairs of a city. 3. A committee.

coun sel /koun′ səl/ *n.* 1. Advice; instruction. *After some thought George followed his parents' counsel.* 2. The act of exchanging ideas. 3. A legal adviser. —*v.* To give advice to.

cou ra geous /kə rā′ jəs/ *adj.* To be full of courage; fearless; brave.

cour te sy /kėr′ tə sē/ *n., pl.* COURTESIES. 1. Polite behavior shown to others. *Barbara sent a thank-you note as an act of courtesy.* 2. A courteous act or expression.

crest fall en /krest′ fô′ lən/ *adj.* Discouraged; disheartened. *Maria was crestfallen when she heard that the weekend trip had been canceled.*

crim i nal /krim′ ə nəl/ *n.* A person who has been found guilty of a crime; a convict.

crit i cize /krit′ ə sīz/ *v.,* CRITICIZED, CRITICIZING. 1. To find fault with; to blame. *Do not criticize unless you can make suggestions for improvement.* 2. To act as a judge.

cul ti vate /kul′ tə vāt/ *v.,* CULTIVATED, CULTIVATING. 1. To till the soil. *A farmer needs various kinds of machines to cultivate the fields.* 2. To improve and develop by study.

cul ture /kul′ chər/ *n.* 1. The civilization of a people at a given time. *The culture of ancient Egypt was distinguished by some amazing developments in the arts and crafts.* 2. The preparation of land. 3. The result of good training and schooling. 4. A growth or colony of germs prepared for scientific study or experiment. [French *culture*]

cur i ous /kyùr′ ē əs/ *adj.* 1. Eager to know. *She is an unusually curious child.* 2. Inquisitive; prying. 3. Odd.

cus to dy /kus′ tə dē/ *n., pl.* CUSTODIES. Possession; care. *The diamonds will remain in the custody of the court until further notice.* [Latin *custodia*]

cus tom /kus′ təm/ *n.* 1. A usual practice or procedure. *In England it is the custom to drive on the left side of the road.* 2. A personal habit.

cy cle /sī′ kəl/ *n.* 1. A predictable series of events. *How many steps are there in the life cycle of a butterfly?* 2. A period of time. —*v.,* CYCLED, CYCLING. To travel by bicycle, tricycle, or motorcycle.

D

dan ger ous /dān′ jər əs *or* dānj′ rəs/ *adj.* Unsafe; risky; hazardous.

dec ade /dek′ ād *or* dek′ əd/ *n.* A group of ten, particularly a period of ten years.

de ceased /di sēst′/ *n.* A dead person. *They read the will of the deceased.* — *adj.* Dead.

de cent /dē′ sənt/ *adj.* **1.** Fit and proper; appropriate according to circumstances. *It is not decent to whistle in class.* **2.** Fairly good, but not excellent.

de cep tion /di sep′ shən/ *n.* The act of leading someone to believe something that is not true. *The child's deception in forging the signature was discovered by the bank teller.*

dec i mal /des′ ə məl/ *adj.* Pertaining to the number system based on ten, in which each value position, or place, represents a value ten times as large as the one at its right and one-tenth as large as the one at its left. *He gave the answer .5, which is a decimal number.* — *n.* A decimal number or fraction.

de ci sion /di sizh′ ən/ *n.* **1.** The act of making up one's mind. *How did you happen to come to that decision?* **2.** A fixed and final opinion. **3.** Firmness; determination.

de ci sive /di sī′ siv/ *adj.* **1.** Deciding. *Anthony's testimony was the decisive factor in changing our minds.* **2.** Conclusive; final.

dec la ra tion /dek′ lə rā′ shən/ *n.* A strong positive statement. *Our class made a public declaration against cheating.*

de fine /di fīn′/ *v.,* DEFINED, DEFINING. To give the meaning of; to explain.

def i nite /def′ ə nit/ *adj.* Clear; unmistakable in meaning. *The senator made a definite statement that she would not be a candidate in the next election.*

de flate /di flāt′/ *v.,* DEFLATED, DEFLATING. **1.** To let the air or gas out of something. *The small nail was enough to deflate the tire.* **2.** To lower the importance of.

del i cate /del′ ə kit/ *adj.* **1.** Mildly or subtly pleasing to the senses. *The burning incense has a delicate fragrance.* **2.** Being of fine weave or quality. **3.** Demanding great care, skill, or tact.

de li cious /di lish′ əs/ *adj.* Giving delight or keen pleasure, especially to the sense of taste or smell.

dem on strate /dem′ ən strāt/ *v.,* DEMONSTRATED, DEMONSTRATING. **1.** To show clearly; to prove. *The new figures demonstrate a rise in living costs.* **2.** To explain or show how something is done by performing experiments or using samples. **3.** To express one's feelings openly. **4.** To participate in a public parade or meeting to protest or make demands.

de nom i na tor /di nom′ ə nā′ tər/ *n.* In a fraction, the figure below the line that tells into how many equal parts a thing has been divided.

de ny /di nī′/ *v.,* DENIED, DENYING. **1.** To contradict; to declare to be untrue. *How can you deny that they were here at nine o'clock?* **2.** To refuse to grant. **3.** To disown.

de pend ence /di pen′ dəns/ *n.* Reliance on another person or thing for help or support. *Little Betty placed dependence on her older sister for all her decisions.*

de pot /dē′ pō/ *n., pl.* DEPOTS /dē′ pōz/. A railroad or bus station.

de prive /di prīv′/ *v.,* DEPRIVED, DEPRIVING. To take away from; to put an end to. *Mother had to deprive Bob of the privilege of watching TV until his grades improved.*

de scent /di sent′/ *n.* **1.** The act of going or coming from a higher to a lower place. *We watched the descent of the plane.* **2.** The handing down from parent to child.

---

hat, āge, fär; let, ēqual, tèrm; it, īce; hot, ōpen, ȯrder; oil, out; cup, pu̇t, rüle; ch, child; ng, long; sh, she; th, thin; ᴛʜ, then; zh, measure; ə represents *a* in about, *e* in taken, *i* in pencil, *o* in lemon, *u* in circus.

de scrip tion /di skrip′ shən/ *n.* A word picture. *The officer asked for a **description** of the lost child.*

de spair /di sper′ *or* di spar′/ *v.* To give up hope. *After thirteen days without food or water, the survivors of the crash were beginning to **despair** of ever being rescued.— n.* Hopelessness.

des pe ra do /des′ pə rä′ dō *or* des′ pə rā′ dō/ *n., pl.* DESPERADOS *or* DESPERADOES. A reckless outlaw, usually considered dangerous. *It took four officers to hold back the **desperado**.* [Spanish *desperado*]

des per ate /des′ pər it *or* des′ prit/ *adj.* **1.** Without hope. *At the end of five days, the workers trapped in the mine grew **desperate**.* **2.** Reckless.

de spise /di spīz′/ *v.,* DESPISED, DESPISING. **1.** To scorn; to consider low, mean, and unworthy. *I **despise** cowardice.* **2.** To look down upon.

des sert /di zėrt′/ *n.* Sweets, fruits, or any similar food served at the end of a meal.

des ti na tion /des′ tə nā′shən/ *n.* The place or point to which a person is going or to which something is being sent. *We are still five miles from our **destination**.*

de struc tion /di struk′ shən/ *n.* **1.** The act of destroying; the tearing down of a thing. *The **destruction** of that town was caused by a tornado.* **2.** That which has been destroyed.

de tract /di trakt′/ *v.* To take away. *The old garage in the backyard **detracted** from the beauty of the property.*

di a gram /dī′ ə gram/ *n.* A drawing or illustration that shows the important parts of something. *The coach drew a **diagram** to illustrate the defensive play.—v.* To draw or sketch a picture of something.

di al /dī′ əl/ *n.* **1.** An instrument used for turning on a radio or television set. *The **dial** on the radio seems to be broken.* **2.** An instrument on a telephone used in making a telephone call. **3.** The face of a clock, a gauge, or any similar instrument.

die sel /dē′ zəl/ *n.* An engine in which the mixture of fuel and air is ignited by compressed air. *This long freight is pulled by a **diesel**.—adj.* Operated by a diesel engine.

dif fer ence /dif′ ər əns *or* dif′ rəns/ *n.* **1.** Dissimilarity. *What is the **difference** between an ostrich and an emu?* **2.** Distinction.

dif fi cult /dif′ ə kult/ *adj.* Hard to do, to manage, or to understand.

dig ni ty /dig′ nə tē/ *n.* **1.** Stateliness of manner; nobleness of bearing. *His **dignity** led us to believe he was a gentleman.* **2.** Quality of being respected.

di lem ma /də lem′ ə/ *n.* A predicament. *I am in a **dilemma**, and I don't know how to resolve it.*

di plo ma /də plō′ mə/ *n.* **1.** An official written record or certificate of graduation from a school or college. *To her the **diploma** was a symbol of four years of careful study.* **2.** A document conferring some privilege or honor.

di rec tor /də rek′ tər *or* dī rek′ tər/ *n.* **1.** A manager. *Who is the **director** of this museum?* **2.** One of a group of persons who set policy for a bank, a corporation, etc.

dis creet /dis krēt′/ *adj.* Showing good judgment; careful in speech and action. *The police officer was extremely **discreet** in questioning the victims of the tragedy.*

dis cre tion /dis kresh′ ən/ *n.* **1.** Prudence or wisdom; good judgment, especially in speech. *You showed **discretion** in your remarks last night.* **2.** Freedom to choose or decide. **3.** Caution.

dis cuss /dis kus′/ *v.* To talk over, considering various points of view.

dis ease /də zēz′/ *n.* **1.** A lack of health; illness. *Scientists continue to study all kinds of **disease**.* **2.** Any particular illness, such as measles or arthritis.

dis guise /dis gīz'/ *v.*, DISGUISED, DISGUISING. To make changes in dress or appearance to hide one's identity or to look like someone else. *The thieves **disguised** themselves as guards and entered the museum.*—*n.* Anything that is used in making such a change.

dis gust /dis gust'/ *v.* To displease or offend strongly. *The team knew that its poor co-operation had **disgusted** the coach.*

dis may /dis mā'/ *v.* **1.** To discourage completely. *The soldiers were all **dismayed** by the news that no help could be sent to them.* **2.** To frighten.

dis miss al /dis mis' əl/ *n.* Discharge; removal; ouster. *We were all surprised to hear of the **dismissal** of the director of the museum.*

dis perse /dis pėrs'/ *v.*, DISPERSED, DISPERS-ING. To scatter. *The police were ordered to **disperse** the crowd.*

dis po si tion /dis' pə zish' ən/ *n.* **1.** A natural bent or tendency; temperament. *One should cultivate a cheerful **disposition**.* **2.** The act of getting rid of or determining the fate of.

dis trib ute /dis trib' yüt/ *v.*, DISTRIBUTED, DIS-TRIBUTING. To give a certain amount to each; to divide among several. *Please **distribute** these pencils to the pupils.*

dis tri bu tion /dis' trə byü' shən/ *n.* The passing out. *Were you there during the **distribution** of awards?*

doc u ment /dok' yə mənt/ *n.* A legal or official paper; any written or printed material giving information as proof of some fact.

do mes tic /də mes' tik/ *adj.* **1.** Belonging to the home, family, or household. *I spent the afternoon cleaning, ironing, and doing other **domestic** chores.* **2.** Pertaining to one's country; not foreign. **3.** Tame, especially describing such animals as the dog, horse, and cat.

doubt ful /dout' fəl/ *adj.* Uncertain; full of doubt. *I feel **doubtful** of the team's ability to handle such opponents.*

drug store /drug' stòr'/ *n.* A shop where medicines, cosmetics, etc., are sold.

E

ear nest /ėr' nist/ *adj.* Pertaining to serious-ness of purpose. *She is making an **earnest** effort to learn to swim.*

ed it /ed'it/ *v.* **1.** To prepare for publication. *We have not yet begun to **edit** Dr. Crowe's manuscript.* **2.** To decide what to print in a publication.

ef fect /ə fekt'/ *n.* **1.** A result. *One **effect** of this medicine will be an increase in your appe-tite.* **2.** An influence.—*v.* To cause to hap-pen.

e lec tric i ty /i lek tris' ə tē/ *n.* A form of ener-gy or source of power used to run motors and devices for lighting, heating, and com-munication.

el o quent /el' ə kwənt/ *adj.* Very expressive. *What an **eloquent** speaker Senator Harvey is!*

em broi der y /em broi' dər ē *or* em broid' rē/ *n.* **1.** The art of stitching designs on fabric or leather. *Do you know how to do em-broidery?* **2.** Embroidered designs on a material.

em er ald /em' ər əld *or* em' rəld/ *n.* A bright-green precious gem. *What a beautiful emer-ald that is!* [French *esmeralde*]

e mer gen cy /i mėr' jən sē/ *n., pl.* EMERGEN-CIES. An unexpected need for prompt ac-tion.

en dure /en dùr' *or* en dyür'/ *v.*, ENDURED, ENDURING. To suffer patiently; to bear. *He could scarcely **endure** the pain.* [French *endurer*]

hat, āge, fär; let, ēqual, tėrm; it, īce; hot, ōpen, òrder; oil, out; cup, pùt, rüle; ch, child; ng, long; sh, she; th, thin; ᴛʜ, then; zh, measure; ə represents *a* in about, *e* in taken, *i* in pencil, *o* in lemon, *u* in circus.

en gi neer /en′ jə nir′/ *n.* **1.** A person who operates an engine. *My uncle is a locomotive* **engineer.** **2.** A person who designs and manages the building of engines, bridges, canals, and the like.

e nor mous /i nôr′ məs/ *adj.* Huge; extremely large.

e ro sion /i rō′ zhən/ *n.* The process of wearing away, especially land by wind or water. *Tons of good topsoil are lost by erosion.*

es pe cial ly /e spesh′ ə lē *or* e spesh′ lē/ *adv.* Particularly; to an unusual degree. *Since he was* **especially** *careful at railroad crossings, we cannot understand how the accident occurred.*

es tab lish /e stab′ lish/ *v.* **1.** To set up; to found or begin. *Did Portugal* **establish** *any colonies in the New World?* **2.** To put on a firm basis.

e val u ate /i val′ yü āt/ *v.,* EVALUATED, EVALUATING. To place a value upon; to appraise. *It was difficult to* **evaluate** *the beautiful antiques.*

e ven tu al ly /i ven′ chü ə lē *or* i ven′ chəl ē/ *adv.* Finally; ultimately; in the end.

ev i dence /ev′ ə dəns/ *n.* **1.** Anything that helps to prove or disprove something. *The lawyer had obtained* **evidence** *in favor of the defendant.* **2.** An indication.

ev i dent ly /ev′ ə dənt lē/ *adv.* Clearly; plainly. **Evidently** *you were expecting someone else.*

ex am i na tion /eg zam′ ə nā′ shən/ *n.* **1.** A test to determine fitness or achievement. *Our* **examination** *in arithmetic took about an hour.* **2.** An investigation.

ex am ine /eg zam′ ən/ *v.,* EXAMINED, EXAMINING. **1.** To inspect carefully. *An inspector will* **examine** *the electric wiring.* **2.** To test.

ex ceed /ek sēd′/ *v.* To go beyond; to be greater than. *The driver had* **exceeded** *the speed limit prescribed by law in that community.*

ex cel lence /ek′ sə ləns/ *n.* Quality; superi- ority. *You should always strive for* **excellence** *in whatever you do.*

ex cep tion /ek sep′ shən/ *n.* **1.** The act of leaving out. *I like all green vegetables, with the* **exception** *of asparagus.* **2.** Someone or something that has been left out.

ex cur sion /ek skėr′ zhən/ *n.* A short journey or trip. *There are special rates for the* **excursion** *to Niagara Falls.*

ex emp tion /eg zemp′ shən/ *n.* Freedom from a duty or release from an obligation. *Mr. Lower was able to claim several* **exemptions** *in filing his income tax report.*

ex hib it /eg zib′ it/ *n.* That which is shown to the public. *At the fair we saw an* **exhibit** *of articles made by seventh graders.*—*v.* To show.

ex pan sion /ek span′ shən/ *n.* **1.** The act or process of growing larger and increasing in size. *The old neighborhood disappeared with the* **expansion** *of the highway.* **2.** Something that has increased in size.

ex pec ta tion /ek′ spek tā′ shən/ *n.* The act or state of looking forward to something.

ex pe di tion /ek′ spə dish′ ən/ *n.* A setting forth for some specific purpose, as in exploration. *A scientific* **expedition** *requires long and careful planning.*

ex pel /ek spel′/ *v.,* EXPELLED, EXPELLING. **1.** To drive out. *We used smoke to* **expel** *the bees from the hive.* **2.** To force to leave.

ex per i ence /ek spir′ ē əns/ *n.* **1.** The event or events one lives through. *His attitude is the result of a sad* **experience** *in his youth.* **2.** Knowledge and ability gained by living through certain events.—*v.,* EXPERIENCED, EXPERIENCING. To live through or undergo.

ex per i ment /ek sper′ ə mənt *or* ek spir′ ə mənt/ *n.* A test performed to prove or disprove something.

ex pert /ek spėrt′ *or* ek′ spėrt′/ *adj.* Skillful; experienced. *She was an* **expert** *skater and hoped to get a professional skating posi-*

tion.—/ek′ spėrt′/ *n.* An authority; a specialist.

ex pla na tion /ek′ splə nā′ shən/ *n.* **1.** The act of making plain. *Sandra said that Bill's explanation of the problem was clear.* **2.** That which clears up any misunderstanding.

ex plor er /ek splôr′ ər/ *n.* One who explores. *Columbus was one of the greatest explorers of all time.*

ex pose /ek spōz′/ *v.,* EXPOSED, EXPOSING. **1.** To reveal. *Who finally exposed the criminal?* **2.** To uncover.

ex ten sion /ek sten′ shən/ *n.* **1.** An addition. *The extension of the highway will soon be completed.* **2.** A stretching out or lengthening.

ex tin guish /ek sting′ gwish/ *v.* To put out or quench. *The fire fighters extinguished the fire.*

ex treme /ek strēm′/ *adj.* Very great; excessive. *The use of gasoline in making fires involves extreme risks.*—*n.* **1.** The very end. **2.** That which is beyond reason.

F

fa cial /fā′ shəl/ *adj.* Pertaining to the face. *I can usually tell what Peter is thinking from his facial expression.*

fare well /fer′ wel′ *or* far′ wel′/ *interj.* An exclamation used in parting which means, "I wish you well." *My friend waved from the dock and shouted, "Farewell!"*—*n.* The act of leaving.

fa vor ite /fā′ vər it *or* fāv′ rit/ *adj.* Looked upon with special affection. *Pumpkin pie is my favorite dessert.*—*n.* The person or thing that is favored most by someone.

fee ble /fē′ bəl/ *adj.* **1.** Weak; lacking in strength. *The patient grew more feeble.* **2.** Lacking in authority or influence.

fic tion /fik′ shən/ *n.* A story which is imagined or made up; not based on facts.

fierce /firs/ *adj.* Savage; violent. *The lion is a fierce animal.*

fie ry /fī′ rē/ *adj.* **1.** Full of intense feeling. *Jim's fiery temper often caused him to do things that he regretted later.* **2.** Flaming; consisting of fire. **3.** Hot.

fir /fėr/ *n.* A conical-shaped evergreen. *The balsam fir is often used as a Christmas tree.*

flat ter y /flat′ ər ē/ *n.* Praise beyond what is true.

fleet /flēt/ *adj.* Rapid; swiftly moving. *The fleet deer escaped from the hunter.*—*n.* **1.** A number of warships under a single commander. **2.** A nation's navy. [Old English *fleotan,* to float]

flu id /flü′ id/ *n.* A liquid. *He noticed that fluid was leaking from the lighter.*—*adj.* Flowing freely, like water.

foot /fut/ *n., pl.* FEET. **1.** The end part of a leg which a person, animal, or object stands on. *The young horse struggled as it rose to its feet.* **2.** That part of an object which is opposite its head. **3.** The lowest part of something; the base or bottom. **4.** A measure of length equal to twelve inches.

for tu nate /fôr′ chə nit/ *adj.* Describing unexpected success. *I was fortunate in being able to get an appointment.*

fra grance /frā′ grəns/ *n.* An agreeable smell. *The fragrance of the lilacs floated through the window to us.*

frank furt er /frangk′ fər tər/ *n.* A kind of sausage. *I asked for mustard on my frankfurter.* [German *Frankfurter,* pertaining to Frankfort, a city in Germany]

fric tion /frik′ shən/ *n.* **1.** The act of rubbing sharply one thing against another. *Matches are lighted by friction.* **2.** Disagreement between persons.

---

hat, āge, fär; let, ēqual, tėrm; it, īce; hot, ōpen, ôrder; oil, out; cup, pùt, rüle; ch, child; ng, long; sh, she; th, thin; ᴛʜ, then; zh, measure; ə represents *a* in about, *e* in taken, *i* in pencil, *o* in lemon, *u* in circus.

fron tier /frun tir'/ *n.* **1.** Largely unexplored territory, just recently having been entered by pioneers. *What new frontier will they explore next?* **2.** The boundary line between two countries.

func tion /fungk' shən/ *n.* **1.** The use or purpose of. *The function of the heart is to pump the blood.* **2.** A formal social event. — *v.* To operate as intended.

fur /fėr/ *n.* The outer covering of mammals. *My new coat is trimmed with rabbits' fur.*

fur i ous /fyür' ē əs/ *adj.* Violent, especially in a rage. *She was furious when she realized how unfair you had been to Christopher.*

G

gal ler y /gal' ər ē *or* gal' rē/ *n., pl.* GALLERIES. **1.** A room for the exhibition of works of art. *Several paintings by Winslow Homer are on exhibit in that gallery.* **2.** A long passage, or hall.

gen ial /jē' nyəl *or* jē' nē əl/ *adj.* Kind; cheerful. *Mr. Crete is a genial host.*

gen ius /jē' nyəs *or* jē' nē əs/ *n., pl.* GENIUSES. **1.** A person having unusual natural ability or talent. *Mendelssohn was a genius in music.* **2.** Intelligence; wisdom.

ge ol o gy /jē ol' ə jē/ *n.* A science that deals with the earth, the rocks of which it is composed, and the changes it has undergone or is undergoing. *Geology, geography, and mathematics are my favorite subjects.* [Latin *geologia*]

glo ri ous /glôr' ē əs/ *adj.* **1.** Full of splendor. *The sunrise was a glorious example of nature's beauty.* **2.** Worthy of glory or praise.

gnaw /nô/ *v.* To wear away by biting small bits with the teeth.

gov er nor /guv' ər nər/ *n.* **1.** The chief executive officer of a state. *This bill must be signed by the governor before it can become a law.* **2.** A ruler.

gra cious /grā' shəs/ *adj.* Courteous and kind. *Our gracious hostess introduced us to her guests.*

grad u a tion /graj' ü ā' shən *or* graj' ə wā'shən/ *n.* The act of finishing a course of study at a school, college, or university and receiving a diploma or similar certificate.

gram mar /gram' ər/ *n.* The study or science of the form and use of words in any given language.

grate ful /grāt' fəl/ *adj.* **1.** Thankful; appreciative. *I am most grateful for the many courtesies you have shown me.* **2.** Giving pleasure and satisfaction.

guess /ges/ *v.* To form an opinion without really knowing the facts. *Guess the number of beans in the jar.* — *n.* An opinion not based on fact.

guest /gest/ *n.* A person who is entertained by another or by an organization.

gym na si um /jim nā' zē əm/ *n.* A building in which athletic exercises and contests take place. *Where is the gymnasium?* [Greek *gymnasion*]

H

ham burg er /ham' bėr' gər/ *n.* **1.** Ground beef. *I like hamburger cooked with onions.* **2.** A sandwich made with ground beef. [German *Hamburger*, pertaining to Hamburg, a city in Germany]

har ass /har' əs *or* hə ras'/ *v.* **1.** To attack swiftly and repeatedly. *All during the retreat the soldiers were harassed by the enemy.* **2.** To annoy; to vex.

hem i sphere /hem' ə sfir/ *n.* Half of a sphere, especially the globe. *The United States is in the northern hemisphere.*

hes i tate /hez' ə tāt/ *v.*, HESITATED, HESITATING. To pause because of uncertainty or doubt.

high school /hī′ skül′/ *n.* In the United States, a school attended after elementary school, preparing pupils for college, business, or a trade. *We have a four-year **high school**.*

his to ri cal /hi stôr′ ə kəl/ *adj.* **1.** Having to do with history. *My mother is a member of the Fall River **Historical** Society.* **2.** True to history, as a historical novel.

hon or ar y /on′ ə rer′ ē/ *adj.* Bestowed as an honor.

ho ri zon /hə rī′ zən/ *n.* **1.** An imaginary line where the earth and sky seem to meet. *The sun was rising on the distant **horizon**.* **2.** The range of a person's thinking, interest, experience, or outlook.

ho ri zon tal /hôr′ ə zon′ təl/ *adj.* **1.** To be parallel to the horizon; to be at right angles to a vertical line. *The children played on the **horizontal** bars.* **2.** Level; flat.

hor ror /hôr′ ər/ *n.* **1.** Terror; excessive fear. *The child has a **horror** of darkness.* **2.** That which causes great fear.

hu man /hyü′ mən/ *adj.* Pertaining to people. *The research report dealt with various aspects of **human** behavior.* — *n.* A person; a human being.

hu man i ty /hyü man′ ə tē/ *n.* **1.** Human nature. *Both kind and unkind acts are characteristic of **humanity**.* **2.** The human race.

hu mor ous /hyü′ mər əs/ *adj.* Full of humor; amusing; funny.

I

i cy /ī′ sē/ *adj.* **1.** Very cold. *The water in the pitcher was **icy**.* **2.** Having ice within or upon [Old English *is*, ice]

i den ti ty /ī den′ tə tē/ *n., pl.* IDENTITIES. Identification; name.

i dle /ī′ dəl/ *adj.* Not busy. *When the mills closed, many workers were **idle**.*

i dol /ī′ dəl/ *n.* **1.** Any person or thing which is loved devotedly. *The great ballerina was the **idol** of all the young dancers.* **2.** An image of a false god which is worshiped.

ig ni tion /ig nish′ ən/ *n.* The process of setting a fuel mixture on fire. *The car won't start because there is something wrong with the **ignition**.*

ig nor ance /ig′ nər əns/ *n.* A want or lack of knowledge.

il lu sion /i lü′ zhən/ *n.* A sight, appearance, or feeling that gives a false impression. *The tiny ceiling lights gave the **illusion** of stars in the sky.*

im age /im′ ij/ *n.* **1.** A mental picture. *From the description you have given, I have a clear **image** of the scene.* **2.** A likeness made of material such as wood or stone. **3.** A copy or counterpart.

i mag i nar y /i maj′ ə ner′ ē/ *adj.* Fancied; unreal. *The doctor told Mrs. Blake that her illness was only **imaginary**.*

im i tate /im′ ə tāt/ *v.,* IMITATED, IMITATING. **1.** To model one's behavior after; to follow the pattern of. *The girl tried to **imitate** the singer's style.* **2.** To copy or repeat something.

im part /im pärt′/ *v.* **1.** To make known. *The professor seemed eager to **impart** her knowledge.* **2.** To share.

in come /in′ kum′/ *n.* Money that comes in from business, labor, property, etc.

in cor po rate /in kôr′ pə rāt′/ *v.,* INCORPORATED, INCORPORATING. **1.** To unite or combine in one body. *I have **incorporated** these facts in my final report.* **2.** To form into a corporation or legal unit.

in de pend ence /in′ di pen′ dəns/ *n.* **1.** Freedom from the support or rule of others. *The United States declared its **independence** in

hat, āge, fär; let, ēqual, tėrm; it, īce; hot, ōpen, ôrder; oil, out; cup, put, rüle; ch, child; ng, long; sh, she; th, thin; ŦH, then; zh, measure; ə represents *a* in about, *e* in taken, *i* in pencil, *o* in lemon, *u* in circus.

1776. **2.** A state of not needing or wanting help from others.

in di cate /in′ də kāt/ *v.*, INDICATED, INDICAT-ING. To show; to point out.

in dus tri ous /in dus′ trē əs/ *adj.* Working steadily; not lazy. *An increase in pay was promised to the industrious boys.*

i ni ti a tion /i nish′ ē ā′ shən/ *n.* A ceremony by which a person is admitted to member-ship in an organization or society.

in no cence /in′ ə səns/ *n.* The state or quality of being free from any wrongdoing. *The suspects were able to prove their innocence in court.*

in no cent /in′ ə sənt/ *adj.* Free from sin or guilt, especially due to ignorance of an in-tended evil; blameless. *The evidence clear-ly proved that the suspect was innocent.*

in spi ra tion /in′ spə rā′ shən/ *n.* An influence arousing the desire to live up to one's high-est possibilities. *I gain inspiration from reading the biography of someone who has overcome difficulties.*

in stru ment /in′ strə mənt/ *n.* **1.** A device or tool used as an aid in doing something. *The dentist's instrument for pulling teeth is called a forceps.* **2.** A device upon which musical sounds are produced.

in su late /in′ sə lāt/ *v.*, INSULATED, INSULAT-ING. To wrap or pack with material to pre-vent leakage of electricity, heat, or sound.

in sur ance /in shur′ əns/ *n.* **1.** Assurance. *The name of this firm on a product is your insur-ance of quality.* **2.** A contract by which one party undertakes for a payment, or pre-mium, to guarantee to another against risk or loss.

in ter i or /in tir′ ē ər/ *n.* **1.** The inside. *The interior of the building had been newly decorated.* **2.** The inland part of a country.— *adj.* Inside; inner.

in ter jec tion /in′ tər jek′ shən/ *n.* **1.** In gram-mar, a part of speech; an exclamation.

"Oh!" is an interjection. **2.** Something in-serted, as a remark.

in ter ven tion /in′ tər ven′ shən/ *n.* The act of interfering, with the aim of settling a dis-pute, a misunderstanding, etc. *The governor hinted that state intervention may become necessary if the strike is not settled soon.*

in vi ta tion /in′ və tā′ shən/ *n.* **1.** An oral or written request to come somewhere or do something. *She received an invitation to become a member of the Nature Club.* **2.** The act of inviting or asking a person.

ir ri gate /ir′ ə gāt/ *v.*, IRRIGATED, IRRIGATING. To supply water to dry land by means of canals and ditches.

ir ri ga tion /ir′ ə gā′ shən/ *n.* The act or pro-cess of watering land by artificial means.

J

jeal ous /jel′ əs/ *adj.* **1.** Envious; fearful lest a rival take one's place. *She was jealous of her sister.* **2.** Watchful, particularly of rights and possessions.

junc tion /jungk′ shən/ *n.* **1.** The act or process of joining or being joined. *The junction of the two highways caused hazardous driving conditions.* **2.** The place where joining or meeting occurs.

K

kin der gar ten /kin′ dər gärt′ ən *or* kin′ dər-gärd′ ən/ *n.* A school for young children, especially in the four to six age group. *Most children attend kindergarten for a year.* [German *Kindergarten*, children's garden]

L

la bel /lā′ bəl/ *n.* A tag; a written or printed slip affixed to anything to denote its contents, ownership, price, destination, etc. *Be sure that there is a **label** on every box before you put it in storage.* — *v.* To affix a label to.

la ser /lā′ zər/ *n.* A device that produces a very narrow, intense beam of light that can be used to cut or melt hard materials, remove diseased body tissues, transmit telephone and television signals, etc.

lib er al /lib′ ər əl *or* lib′ rəl/ *adj.* **1.** Generous. *He was **liberal** in the contribution to the Heart Fund.* **2.** Broad-minded; not strict or narrow in one's views.

lit e rar y /lit′ ə rer′ ē/ *adj.* Pertaining to letters or literature; knowing literature. *He became a librarian because he is interested in **literary** works.*

lit er a ture /lit′ ər ə chůr *or* li′ trə chůr′/ *n.* **1.** Writings of a people or a language that are kept alive. *The English have produced much great **literature**.* **2.** The body of writing on a given subject. **3.** Any kind of printed matter.

lo cal i ty /lō kal′ ə tē/ *n., pl.* LOCALITIES. A region; a place.

loose /lüs/ *adj.* **1.** Not tightly fastened. *The button on Linda's coat was **loose**.* **2.** Free. **3.** Not closely fitted.

lo qua cious /lō kwā′ shəs/ *adj.* Talkative. *Pat is the most **loquacious** person I know.*

lose /lüz/ *v.* To meet with a loss; to be unable to find. *Where did you **lose** your book?*

lunch eon /lun′ chən/ *n.* **1.** A light meal eaten in the middle of the day; lunch. *We have at least one hot dish for **luncheon** each day.* **2.** A formal lunch.

M

mac a ro ni /mak′ ə rō′ nē/ *n.* A type of noodle. *We are going to have **macaroni** and cheese for lunch.*

mag net /mag′ nit/ *n.* **1.** A kind of stone or piece of metal that has the ability to attract iron or steel; a loadstone. *The teacher used a **magnet** to separate the iron filings from the dirt.* **2.** Anything that attracts.

mag net ic /mag net′ ik/ *adj.* Possessing the properties of a magnet.

ma jor i ty /mə jôr′ ə tē/ *n., pl.* MAJORITIES. **1.** More than half. *To be elected she must receive the **majority** of the votes cast.* **2.** The amount by which one number is greater than another. **3.** Legal age.

man sion /man′ shən/ *n.* A house of some size or pretension; a stately residence.

mar gin /mär′ jən/ *n.* A strip around the edge; a border. *Leave a one-inch **margin** on all sides of your paper.*

ma rine /mə rēn′/ *adj.* Having to do with the sea. *The glass-bottomed boat enabled the crew to observe the **marine** creatures.* — *n.* A member of the United States Marines. [Latin *marinus*, of the sea]

mar shal /mär′ shəl/ *n.* **1.** An officer of a court, especially a federal court, corresponding to the sheriff of a county; in some foreign countries, a high military officer. *The United States **marshal** appeared in court.* **2.** A person who arranges the order of a procession. — *v.* To arrange in order.

mar vel /mär′ vəl/ *v.* To wonder at. *I have always **marveled** at the way David can come up with solutions to problems.*

mar vel ous /mär′ və ləs *or* märv′ ləs/ *adj.* Wonderful; almost beyond belief.

me chan ic /mə kan′ ik/ *n.* **1.** A worker skilled in operating or repairing machines. *She is a splendid **mechanic** and will be able to repair the machinery without delay.* **2.** Anyone skilled with tools.

me di a tor /mē′ dē ā′ tər/ *n.* An intercessor; one who goes between two parties to bring

---

hat, āge, fär; let, ēqual, tėrm; it, īce; hot, ōpen, ȯrder; oil, out; cup, pùt, rüle; ch, child; ng, long; sh, she; th, thin; ᴛʜ, then; zh, measure; ə represents *a* in about, *e* in taken, *i* in pencil, *o* in lemon, *u* in circus.

about peace. *The referee acted as **mediator** between the quarreling team captains.*

me lo di ous /mə lō′ dē əs/ *adj.* Pleasing to hear; musical.

mel o dy /mel′ ə dē/ *n., pl.* MELODIES. **1.** A harmonious tune resulting from the arrangement of single tones. *The music box played a familiar **melody**.* **2.** In musical compositions, the main tune as distinguished from the harmony and rhythm.

mer it /mer′ it/ *v.* To deserve because of faithful service or special performance. *The salesclerk **merited** a promotion for the outstanding service.*—*n.* **1.** Worth or excellence. **2.** Deserved reward or punishment.

mil i tar y /mil′ ə ter′ ē/ *adj.* Pertaining to war or to an army and soldiers.

min i a ture /min′ ē ə chùr′, min′ ə chùr′, or min′ yə chùr′/ *adj.* Much smaller than normally; tiny. *Have you seen Albert's **miniature** camera?*

mis er y /miz′ ər ē or miz′ rē/ *n., pl.* MISERIES. Great distress. *The **misery** existing in the tenement district is partly due to overcrowded conditions.*

mis sile /mis′ əl/ *n.* A military rocket. *The engineers are going to test-fire the new **missile** today.*

mod i fy /mod′ ə fī/ *v.,* MODIFIED, MODIFYING. **1.** To change slightly the meaning or form of. *I should like to **modify** that statement.* **2.** To make less severe; to tone down. **3.** In grammar, to limit the meaning of.

mo ral /môr′ əl/ *adj.* **1.** Virtuous in character or conduct. *She lives up to high **moral** principles.* **2.** Pertaining to right and wrong.—*n.* A lesson or hidden truth in a story or event.

mus cle /mus′ əl/ *n.* Tissue in the body which controls movement.

mu se um /myü zē′ əm/ *n.* A building housing historical objects, objects of art, or objects of a natural or scientific nature.

mys ter i ous /mi stir′ ē əs/ *adj.* Filled with mystery; beyond understanding. *Her disappearance was most **mysterious**.*

N

ne go ti a tions /ni gō′ shē ā′ shənz/ *n.* A series of conferences concerning business matters or transactions.

neigh bor hood /nā′ bər hùd/ *n.* Vicinity. *Do you live in this **neighborhood**?*

neu tral /nü′ trəl or nyü′ trəl/ *adj.* **1.** Not favoring either side in a conflict or contest. *The ref found it hard to remain **neutral** as she listened to the argument.* **2.** Having no definite characteristics.

night mare /nīt′ mer′ or nīt′ mar′/ *n.* **1.** A terrifying dream. *Since he awoke screaming, we supposed that he must have had a **nightmare**.* **2.** A distressing experience.

no bil i ty /nō bil′ ə tē/ *n., pl.* NOBILITIES. **1.** Loftiness in character; superiority in conduct. *To serve others in forgetfulness of self is a mark of **nobility**.* **2.** People of high birth, such as princesses, earls, and counts.

nom i nal /nom′ ə nəl/ *adj.* **1.** In name only. *Mr. Bryan is the **nominal** president of our club, but Mr. Silva actually does all the planning and makes all the decisions.* **2.** Very small, as a nominal fee.

nom i nate /nom′ ə nāt/ *v.,* NOMINATED, NOMINATING. **1.** To name a candidate for an office. *Our committee is eager to **nominate** a candidate for the office of class president.* **2.** To appoint.

nu mer ous /nü′ mər əs or nyü′ mər əs/ *adj.* Great in number; many; plentiful.

O

oath /ōth/ *n.* An appeal to God to bear witness to the truth of what one says. *With a solemn **oath**, Mr. Rodgers stated he would tell the truth.* [Old English *ath*]

o be di ence /ō bē′ dē əns/ *n.* Submission to authority. *Try as I might, I could never teach my dog* **obedience.**

ob li ga tion /ob′ lə gā′ shən/ *n.* **1.** A responsibility incurred by reason of indebtedness for a favor or continued favors. *We can never cancel our* **obligation** *to our parents.* **2.** An agreement or promise which binds one.

ob long /ob′ lông/ *adj.* Longer than wide. *Here is an* **oblong** *box for the silverware.*

ob ses sion /əb sesh′ ən/ *n.* An inescapable feeling or idea that takes up all one's attention. *What began as a hobby turned out to be an* **obsession.**

ob vi ous /ob′ vē əs/ *adj.* Plainly evident; needing no proof.

oc ca sion /ə kā′ zhən/ *n.* **1.** A timely opportunity. *Your visit gives us an* **occasion** *to hear about your vacation.* **2.** A particular set of circumstances which serves as the cause of something. **3.** An unusual event.

oc cu py /ok′ yə pī/ *v.*, OCCUPIED, OCCUPYING. **1.** To dwell in. *The Smiths now* **occupy** *their own house.* **2.** To employ or keep busy.

oc cur /ə kėr′/ *v.*, OCCURRED, OCCURRING. **1.** To happen or take place. *Tornadoes sometimes* **occur** *in the Southwest.* **2.** To come to mind.

oc cur rence /ə kėr′ əns/ *n.* An event; a happening.

or ches tra /ôr′ kə strə/ *n.* **1.** A group of performers on various musical instruments, especially stringed instruments. *The* **orchestra** *played the overture to the opera.* **2.** The part of the theater or hall used by the musicians; the space just in front of the stage.

or di nar y /ôrd′ ən er′ ē *or* ôrd′ ner ē/ *adj.* Common; not exceptional or distinguished.

or gan i za tion /ôr′ gə nə zā′ shən/ *n.* **1.** A group of persons united for some special purpose. *An* **organization** *usually has a president, a secretary, and a treasurer.* **2.** The orderly arrangement of parts or persons in relation to one another in the interest of efficiency.

o ri gin /ôr′ ə jin/ *n.* The source or beginning. *The* **origin** *of her trouble was poor study habits.*

o rig i nal /ə rij′ ə nəl/ *adj.* **1.** First in order of existence. *The* **original** *price of the sofa had been reduced by 40%.* **2.** Newly created or thought of. **3.** Inventive.—*n.* The first or real example from which others are copied.

or phan /ôr′ fən/ *n.* A child whose parents are dead.

o ver coat /ō′ vər kōt′/ *n.* A heavy outer coat worn in cold weather.

ox y gen /ok′ sə jən/ *n.* A tasteless, colorless, and odorless gas. *People must have* **oxygen** *to live.* [French *oxygène*]

P

pan el /pan′ əl/ *n.* **1.** A section of a wall or other surface which is marked off in some way to distinguish it from the surface as a whole. *We painted the* **panel** *pale blue.* **2.** A number of persons chosen to serve in some special way.—*v.* To decorate with panels.

par a chute /par′ ə shüt/ *n.* An umbrella-shaped device, usually made of nylon or silk, used in descending through the air from great heights. *The skydiver performed a daring free fall before she opened her* **parachute.**—*v.*, PARACHUTED, PARACHUTING. To land by means of a parachute.

par al lel /par′ ə lel/ *adj.* **1.** Lying or extending in the same direction and equidistant from one another at all points. *A railroad track consists of* **parallel** *rails.* **2.** With like purpose or meaning.

---

hat, āge, fär; let, ēqual, tėrm; it, īce; hot, ōpen, ôrder; oil, out; cup, pùt, rüle; ch, child; ng, long; sh, she; th, thin; ᴛʜ, then; zh, measure; ə represents *a* in about, *e* in taken, *i* in pencil, *o* in lemon, *u* in circus.

par cel post /pär′ səl pōst′/ *n.* That part of the postal service which receives, sends, and delivers parcels. *The charges on parcel post are different from those on letters.*

par tic u lar /pər tik′ yə lər/ *adj.* **1.** Pertaining to one person or thing. *At home each member of the family has particular work to do.* **2.** Considered separately. **3.** Difficult to please. — *n.* A detail.

pa tience /pā′ shəns/ *n.* Leniency; forbearance; perseverance; endurance. *My mother has more patience than any other person I know.*

pa tron /pā′ trən/ *n.* **1.** One who supports, guards, and protects the work and professional name of others; a benefactor. *Lorenzo de Medici, a prince of Florence, Italy, was a patron of artists and writers.* **2.** A customer or client. **3.** A guardian or protector.

pen guin /pen′ gwin/ *n.* A flightless aquatic bird found only in the antarctic regions of the Southern Hemisphere.

pe nin su la /pə nin′ sə lə/ *n.* A body of land extending out into the water. *The state of Florida is a peninsula, and so is the country of Italy.* [Latin *paeninsula*]

pen sion /pen′ shən/ *n.* A stated amount of money paid regularly to a person in recognition of long service, special service, or for injuries sustained in service.

per form ance /pər fôr′ məns/ *n.* **1.** An accomplishment. *I was proud of your performance as a driver in heavy traffic.* **2.** The act of carrying out or completing something. **3.** A public exhibition.

per i gee /per′ ə jē/ *n.* The point in the orbit of a spacecraft when the spacecraft is nearest the earth. *An orbiting spacecraft registers its fastest speed at perigee.*

per suade /pər swād′/ *v.*, PERSUADED, PERSUADING. To influence or convince by argument or advice.

per sua sion /pər swā′ zhən/ *n.* The act of persuading. *Through artful persuasion, David convinced the judges to accept our entry.*

pho tog ra phy /fə tog′ rə fē/ *n.* The process of obtaining images on a sensitive film or plate by the action of light.

phrase /frāz/ *n.* A short expression. *I tried to cut out of my essay every unnecessary phrase.* — *v.*, PHRASED, PHRASING. To express in words.

phy si cian /fə zish′ ən/ *n.* A doctor. *To become a physician, one must have years of training.*

pic co lo /pik′ ə lō/ *n., pl.* PICCOLOS. A small flute which produces a shrill tone an octave higher than that of an ordinary flute.

pig eon /pij′ ən/ *n.* Any of several varieties of domestic birds of the dove family.

pi lot /pī′ lət/ *n.* **1.** One who steers a ship or an airship. *The pilot is responsible for the safety of the craft and passengers.* **2.** A person specially qualified to guide ships in and out of narrow or shallow harbors. — *v.* To guide or lead.

pitch er /pich′ ər/ *n.* **1.** One who pitches or throws anything. *Dot was the pitcher for our baseball team.* **2.** A container used for holding and pouring fluids.

plain /plān/ *adj.* Clear or easy to understand. *The directions were very plain.* — *n.* A flat region.

plane /plān/ *n.* **1.** An airplane. *Uncle Dick flies his own plane.* **2.** A flat surface. **3.** A tool.

plas ter /plas′ tər/ *n.* **1.** A mixture of lime, water, and sand applied when wet to walls and ceilings. *The plaster will harden in two days.* **2.** In medicine, an external application spread on cloth and used to protect, heal, or soothe an injured part of the body. — *v.* **1.** To cover with plaster. **2.** To spread over thickly.

pla teau /pla tō′/ *n.* A flat area high above sea level. *The White River Plateau is in Colorado.* [French *plateau*]

pleas ant /plez′ ənt/ *adj.* Giving pleasure; pleasing; agreeable.

pli ers /plī′ ərz/ *n.* A tool used for bending or grasping objects. *I need the **pliers** to bend this wire.*

plumb er /plum′ ər/ *n.* A worker who installs and repairs pipes and plumbing.

pol i cy /pol′ ə sē/ *n., pl.* POLICIES. **1.** A plan or line of action in a particular situation. *The people in the living room were discussing our country's foreign **policy**.* **2.** A certificate or contract of insurance.

pol i tics /pol′ ə tiks/ *n.* **1.** The science of government. *Politics is a subject I wish to study thoroughly.* **2.** The control or management of public affairs.

pol len /pol′ ən/ *n.* The yellow, powdery dust in flowers.

por tion /pôr′ shən/ *n.* A part; a share. *Peggy ate her **portion** of corned beef and cabbage quickly.*

pos ses sion /pə zesh′ ən/ *n.* **1.** Ownership. *The painting came into my **possession** purely by accident.* **2.** A piece of personal property.

post pone /pōst pōn′/ *v.,* POSTPONED, POSTPONING. To delay; to put off until a later time.

post script /pōst′ skript/ *n.* A part added to a completed letter or book. *I will read you the **postscript** I have written.*

po tion /pō′ shən/ *n.* A drink; a liquid dose. *He claimed that the **potion** would make anyone who drank it invisible.*

pov er ty /pov′ ər tē/ *n.* **1.** The state of being poor. *Abraham Lincoln spent his youth in **poverty**.* **2.** Lack of essentials.

pre cise ly /pri sīs′ lē/ *adv.* Definitely; exactly. *The captain's order was to embark **precisely** at three o'clock.*

pre ci sion /pri sizh′ ən/ *n.* Accuracy; exactness. *The team learned to carry out the new play with **precision**.*

pref er ence /pref′ ər əns/ *n.* **1.** The state of liking or favoring. *Jean's **preference** for the color blue influenced her to choose the blue coat.* **2.** That which is liked better.

pre mi um /prē′ mē əm/ *n.* **1.** A prize; a reward. *The pupil who sells the most magazines will receive a **premium**.* **2.** An amount above the nominal value.

prep o si tion /prep′ ə zish′ ən/ *n.* A part of speech showing direction, time, or position. *The words* by, in, at, *and* with *are common **prepositions**.*

pres sure /presh′ ər/ *n.* **1.** The force of something that is pushing on something else. *The **pressure** of the heavy machine broke the floor.* **2.** A burden or difficulty. **3.** The responsibility of urgent duties.—*v.,* PRESSURED, PRESSURING. To force or exert pressure on.

pre ven tion /pri ven′ shən/ *n.* The act of making something impossible; hindrance.

pre view /prē′ vyü′/ *n.* A showing of part of a movie, a revealing of part of a plan, etc., which gives some indication of what the whole movie or the whole plan, etc., will be.

pre vi ous /prē′ vē əs/ *adj.* Earlier in time; former. *His **previous** record was better than the one he made today.*

prin ci pal /prin′ sə pəl/ *n.* **1.** The head of a school. *The **principal** called the teachers together for a short meeting.* **2.** The chief or head person. **3.** One who takes a leading part. **4.** Money on which interest is being paid.—*adj.* Greatest in importance.

prin ci ple /prin′ sə pəl/ *n.* A fundamental truth; a basic law; a doctrine. *According to the **principle** of home rule, each district will manage its own affairs.*

---

hat, āge, fär; let, ēqual, tėrm; it, īce; hot, ōpen, ôrder; oil, out; cup, pùt, rüle; ch, child; ng, long; sh, she; th, thin; ŦH, then; zh, measure; ə represents *a* in about, *e* in taken, *i* in pencil, *o* in lemon, *u* in circus.

priv i lege /priv′ ə lij *or* priv′ lij/ *n.* A right or favor which is granted, usually offering some special advantage. *All students had the privilege of discount prices.*

pro ceed /prə sēd′ *or* prō sēd′/ *v.* **1.** To move forward. *We proceeded on our journey.* **2.** To come forth.

pro ces sion /prə sesh′ ən/ *n.* A parade or group of people moving forward in an orderly manner.

pro fes sor /prə fes′ ər/ *n.* One who practices or teaches a branch of knowledge in a secondary school, college, or university.

pro fi cient /prə fish′ ənt/ *adj.* Skilled; expert. *Willa has become quite proficient at taking shorthand.*

prof it /prof′ it/ *n.* That which is gained. *Find your profit by deducting your expenses from the amount you took in.—v.* To gain benefit.

pro gres sion /prə gresh′ ən/ *n.* **1.** A moving forward or going ahead. *The long trailer made a slow progression along the narrow mountain road.* **2.** In mathematics, a series of numbers such as 2, 4, 6, 8, 10, etc., in which there is always the same relationship between a number and the one that follows it.

pro jec tion /prə jek′ shən/ *n.* **1.** A part of something that projects or sticks out; an extension. *The climbers successfully maneuvered around the rocky projection.* **2.** The act of throwing or casting forward.

pron to /pron′ tō/ *adv.* Quickly; promptly. *The manager had the man ushered out of the theater pronto.* [Spanish *pronto*]

proph et /prof′ it/ *n.* **1.** A person who predicts what will happen in the future. *The prophet foresaw an earthquake in the area.* **2.** A person who teaches what he believes has been revealed to him by God.

pro por tion /prə pôr′ shən/ *n.* **1.** The relation of one part to another in size. *The picture is long in proportion to its height.* **2.** Balance or symmetry. **3.** An equal or just share. **4.** A mathematical statement of equality between two ratios.

pros per ous /pros′ pər əs *or* pros′ prəs/ *adj.* Successful in every respect; fortunate; thriving. *Her family is prosperous.*

pro tec tion /prə tek′ shən/ *n.* **1.** The act of keeping someone or something from harm. *Fasten the seat belt for your own protection.* **2.** A thing or person who prevents harm.

pul ley /pùl′ ē/ *n.* A wheel with a grooved rim through which a rope passes, used for hoisting or lifting.

pur chase /pėr′ chəs/ *n.* **1.** The act of buying. *The purchase of a suitable hat often requires considerable time.* **2.** That which is bought.—*v.*, PURCHASED, PURCHASING. To buy.

pyr a mid /pir′ ə mid/ *n.* A solid having a four-sided base and triangles for its sides. *We built a pyramid out of snow.* [Latin *pyramis*]

Q

qual i fy /kwol′ ə fī/ *v.*, QUALIFIED, QUALIFYING. To prove that one is fit or capable of doing something.

qual i ty /kwol′ ə tē/ *n., pl.* QUALITIES. **1.** A characteristic. *A quality that I admire is humility.* **2.** Something unusual or special about a person or thing. **3.** The grade of a product.

quan ti ty /kwon′ tə tē/ *n., pl.* QUANTITIES. **1.** An amount. *What quantity of paper should be ordered for the printing of this book?* **2.** A large amount or number.

qui et /kwī′ ət/ *v.* To calm. *The keepers worked hard to quiet the animals during the thunderstorm.—adj.* **1.** Silent; still. **2.** Peaceful.

quite /kwīt/ *adv.* **1.** Entirely. *You are **quite** right.* **2.** Rather; very.

quiz /kwiz/ *n., pl.* QUIZZES. A test. *Our teacher is going to give us a **quiz** today.*—*v.,* QUIZZED, QUIZZING. To test.

R

ra di a tor /rā′ dē ā′ tər/ *n.* That which sends out rays, especially of heat or light.

real es tate /rē′ əl e stāt′ *or* rēl′ e stāt′/ *n.* Property in land or houses. *He paid a high tax on his **real estate.***

reb el[1] /reb′ əl/ *n.* One who fights against the government or other authority. *The **rebels** had planned their uprising for many months.*

re bel[2] /ri bel′/ *v.,* REBELLED, REBELLING. To fight against the government or other authority. *The angry prisoners decided to **rebel.***

re bel lion /ri bel′ yən/ *n.* A revolt against authority. *A long time ago the nobles of Europe rose in **rebellion** against their rulers.*

re cep tion /ri sep′ shən/ *n.* **1.** The act of receiving. *I felt greatly honored by the warm **reception.*** **2.** A social occasion for the purpose of receiving and welcoming people.

reck on /rek′ ən/ *v.* **1.** To calculate; to estimate; to count. *Can you **reckon** the cost of this item?* **2.** To consider; to judge.

re claim /ri klām′/ *v.* To bring or restore land to productive use. *We are trying to **reclaim** this barren, unproductive land from the desert.*

rec og nize /rek′ əg nīz/ *v.,* RECOGNIZED, RECOGNIZING. **1.** To notice and show appreciation for something. *How shall we **recognize** the gift to our club from one of its former members?* **2.** To acknowledge acquaintance with; to remember. **3.** To agree to deal with. **4.** To identify; to perceive.

rec re a tion /rek′ rē ā′ shən/ *n.* **1.** A diversion from labor. *One should choose **recreation** which is quite different from one's work.* **2.** Play.

re cur /ri kėr′/ *v.,* RECURRED, RECURRING. To occur or happen again. *The same spelling errors **recur** often during the year.*

re cur rent /ri kėr′ ənt/ *adj.* Occurring or happening again and again. *We must build a dam to control the **recurrent** floods.*

ref er ence /ref′ ər əns/ *n.* **1.** A statement in writing telling the qualifications of a person applying for employment; a written recommendation. *I will ask my teachers to mail you some **references.*** **2.** A person in position to give information about another's ability or character. **3.** Words directing attention to something else.

reg is ter /rej′ ə stər/ *v.* To enroll; to place one's name on an official list. *Parents will **register** their children for kindergarten.*—*n.* A book in which to keep records.

rein /rān/ *n.* The part of a harness by which a horse is controlled. *When you ride a horse, hold the **reins** loosely.*

rein deer /rān′ dir′/ *n., pl.* REINDEER OR REINDEERS. A kind of deer found in northern countries. *Have you ever seen a **reindeer?*** [Scandinavian *hreindyr*]

re late /ri lāt′/ *v.,* RELATED, RELATING. **1.** To tell about or to give an account of. *The astronaut was asked to **relate** his experiences on the moon.* **2.** To connect or compare in thought or meaning.

rel a tive /rel′ ə tiv/ *adj.* **1.** Pertaining to or connected with. *Here is some information **relative** to your proposed trip.* **2.** Comparative.—*n.* A kinsman.

re li ance /ri lī′ əns/ *n.* Trusting dependence.

---

hat, āge, fär; let, ēqual, tėrm; it, īce; hot, ōpen, òrder; oil, out; cup, pùt, rüle; ch, child; ng, long; sh, she; th, thin; ᴛʜ, then; zh, measure; ə represents *a* in about, *e* in taken, *i* in pencil, *o* in lemon, *u* in circus.

*You can place your **reliance** on this kind of seat belt.*

re lieve /ri lēv′/ *v.*, RELIEVED, RELIEVING. **1.** To free from burden. *I will get a porter to **relieve** you of that heavy suitcase.* **2.** To lessen; to make easier to bear.

rem e dy /rem′ ə dē/ *n., pl.* REMEDIES. **1.** Any medicine, appliance, or treatment that cures a disease or helps to relieve the discomfort of an ailment. *My doctor told me that there is no perfect **remedy** for the common cold.* **2.** That which makes right; that which counteracts any evil or repairs loss. —*v.*, REMEDIED, REMEDYING. To cure; to make right or well.

re mit tance /ri mit′ əns/ *n.* **1.** Money sent in payment. *Her **remittance** came with her letter.* **2.** The act of paying.

rep tile /rep′ təl *or* rep′ tīl/ *n.* An animal that creeps or crawls on its belly or on very short legs.

rep u ta tion /rep′ yə tā′ shən/ *n.* A person's standing in the opinion of those who know him.

res er va tion /rez′ ər vā′ shən/ *n.* An arrangement by which something is held back or set aside for the use of a particular person or persons at a certain time.

res i dence /rez′ ə dəns/ *n.* **1.** A dwelling or place. *She was born and reared in that stone **residence** on the corner.* **2.** The act of residing in a place.

re strain /ri strān′/ *v.* To keep back or hold back. *The puppy was **restrained** from dashing out into the street.*

re strict /ri strikt′/ *v.* To limit. *Did the doctor **restrict** your diet?*

re veal /ri vēl′/ *v.* To uncover; to make known. *None of the conspirators ever **revealed** the name of their leader.*

rev e nue /rev′ ə nü *or* rev′ ə nyü/ *n.* **1.** Income. *The **revenue** from that piece of property is far more than it was ten years ago.*

2. The various kinds of taxes and customs which the government collects.

re view /ri vyü′/ *v.* To look at again carefully. *Did you **review** your words in preparation for the test tomorrow?*

rhyme /rīm/ *n.* **1.** A word or line that ends in the same sound as another word or line. *The word things **rhymes** with the word kings.* **2.** A verse in which similar sounds are repeated, usually at the ends of the lines. —*v.*, RHYMED, RHYMING. To end in the same sound.

rip-roar ing /rip′ rôr′ ing *or* rip′ rōr′ ing/ *adj.* Lively; hilarious. *We had a **rip-roaring** good time at the 4th of July celebration.*

rob /rob/ *v.*, ROBBED, ROBBING. To take something from someone unlawfully and by force. *Did he **rob** the bank?*

rob ber y /rob′ ər ē/ *n., pl.* ROBBERIES. The act of taking something from someone unlawfully and by force.

ro bot /rō′ bät′ *or* rō′ bət/ *n.* **1.** A machine made to look like a human being. *Have you seen the **robot** Mr. Cowles made?* **2.** A machine that performs work automatically. [Czech *robota*, slave labor]

ro de o /rō′ dē ō *or* rō dā′ ō/ *n., pl.* RODEOS. **1.** A public exhibition of some of the skills of cowhands. *The Texas cowhands won the first three prizes at the **rodeo.*** **2.** A cattle round-up [Spanish *rodeo*]

ro tate /rō′ tāt/ *v.*, ROTATED, ROTATING. **1.** To turn in a circle around an axis. *If the earth did not **rotate**, we would not have night and day.* **2.** To use in turn in a fixed order. **3.** To cause to grow in succession, as to rotate crops.

rough neck /ruf′ nek′/ *n.* A rough and often rowdy person. *Little Paul was a **roughneck** when he couldn't go outside and play.*

rub ber neck /rub′ ər nek′/ *v. Slang.* To stretch the neck in order to get a better view. *A crowd stood at the hotel entrance **rubber-***

necking, *hoping to catch a glimpse of the President as he came by.* —*n.* A tourist, especially one on a sightseeing tour.

ru mor /rü′ mər/ *n.* Common talk; current talk which may or may not be true. *There has been a* **rumor** *of bankruptcy for several months.* —*v.* To circulate by talk.

rur al /rür′ əl/ *adj.* Pertaining to the country as distinguished from towns and cities.

S

sal ar y /sal′ ər ē *or* sal′ rē/ *n., pl.* SALARIES. Wages; regular payment for work one is employed to do.

sat is fac tor y /sat′is fak′ tər ē/ *adj.* **1.** Of sufficient quantity or quality to meet a need or demand. *Cotton is one of the most* **satisfactory** *materials for summer clothing.* **2.** Fair; moderate.

sat is fy /sat′is fī/ *v.,* SATISFIED, SATISFYING. **1.** To fulfill a need; to give enough. *The first sandwich Bob ate did not* **satisfy** *him.* **2.** To make amends. **3.** To convince; to assure.

sau cer /sô′ sər/ *n.* A small shallow dish on which to set a cup.

sauer kraut /sour′ krout′/ *n.* A kind of cabbage which has been finely cut, salted, and allowed to sour. *Sauerkraut and sausage is a favorite meal at our house.* [German *Sauerkraut,* sour cabbage]

scar /skär/ *n.* A mark usually as the result of a healed cut, burn, or other injury. *The little boy had a small* **scar** *on his cheek.* —*v.,* SCARRED, SCARRING. To make a scar.

scen er y /sē′ nər ē *or* sēn′ rē/ *n., pl.* SCENER-IES. **1.** Painted scenes used on the stage to represent real places. *The* **scenery** *for the class play was designed by the art classes.* **2.** The general appearance of a landscape.

schol ar /skol′ ər/ *n.* A student of exceptional learning.

sci en tif ic /sī′ ən tif′ ik/ *adj.* Based on the laws of science.

scorch /skôrch/ *v.* **1.** To burn slightly. *I almost* **scorched** *my hand in the fire.* **2.** To dry up; to sear. [Scandinavian *skorpna,* to dry up]

scrump tious /skrump′ shəs *or* skrum′ shəs/ *adj. Slang.* Delicious; elegant. *The mother had prepared a* **scrumptious** *meal for her daughter's homecoming.*

se cur i ty /si kyür′ ə tē/ *n., pl.* SECURITIES. **1.** The state or feeling of being safe. *Our greatest need is emotional* **security.** **2.** That which secures or gives protection. **3.** A bond or stock certificate.

seize /sēz/ *v.,* SEIZED, SEIZING. **1.** To take by force; to take possession of by legal action. *The army expects to* **seize** *the island before the end of the week.* **2.** To grab; to take quickly. **3.** To understand thoroughly.

se lec tion /si lek′ shən/ *n.* Choice. *The cafeteria offered a wide* **selection** *of tempting desserts.*

sen ate /sen′ it/ *n.* A legislative or deliberative body.

sen a tor /sen′ ə tər/ *n.* A member of a senate. *Do you know who your state* **senator** *is?*

sense /sens/ *n.* **1.** Sound judgment; reasonableness. *The solution to the problem requires common* **sense.** **2.** Any one of the five senses: sight, hearing, taste, smell, and touch. **3.** An inner feeling, such as shame or pride. —*v.,* SENSED, SENSING. To perceive; to feel; to understand.

ser i al /sir′ ē əl/ *n.* A story appearing in a series of parts. *That television* **serial** *had been running for several years.*

ses sion /sesh′ ən/ *n.* **1.** The meeting of a court, legislature, or other deliberative body. *The next* **session** *of the court will be*

---

hat, āge, fär; let, ēqual, tėrm; it, īce; hot, ōpen, ôrder; oil, out; cup, pùt, rüle; ch, child; ng, long; sh, she; th, thin; � then; zh, measure; ə represents *a* in about, *e* in taken, *i* in pencil, *o* in lemon, *u* in circus.

held soon. **2.** The period during which a school conducts classes.

shal low /shal′ ō/ *adj.* **1.** Not deep. *The water is **shallow** at this point and is quite safe for wading.* **2.** Unable or unwilling to think deeply; trifling.

sham poo /sham pü′/ *v.* To wash the hair. *I will help you **shampoo** your hair.* —*n., pl.* SHAMPOOS. **1.** The act of shampooing the hair. **2.** The preparation used in shampooing the hair. [Hindu *champo*, press]

sher iff /sher′ if/ *n.* Chief law-enforcing officer of a county.

shin dig /shin′ dig/ *n. Slang.* A social get-together; a party. *The town held a big **shindig** to celebrate the home team's victory.*

shrewd /shrüd/ *adj.* Clever; sharp-witted; cunning; keen. *You will get a **shrewd** answer from John.*

shriek /shrēk/ *n.* A shrill cry. *We heard a **shriek** from someone who saw the mouse.*—*v.* To utter a scream.

siege /sēj/ *n.* A continued effort to take possession or control of something, especially by an army. *The **siege** lasted six weeks.*

sil ver ware /sil′ vər wer′ *or* sil′ vər war′/ *n.* Things made of silver, especially table utensils.

sim plic i ty /sim plis′ ə tē/ *n., pl.* SIMPLICITIES. **1.** Plainness resulting from a lack of ornaments. *The **simplicity** of her dress was becoming.* **2.** The quality or state of being easy to understand. **3.** A lack of cunning.

sin cere ly /sin sir′ lē/ *adv.* Honestly; genuinely; truly.

sing /sing/ *v.* To make musical sounds with the voice.

singe /sinj/ *v.,* SINGED, SINGEING. **1.** To scorch; to burn slightly. *The cook will **singe** the dressed turkey to remove the fine pinfeathers on its skin.* **2.** To burn the ends or outside of something. [Old English *sengan,* to burn lightly]

sin gu lar /sing′ gyə lər/ *adj.* **1.** Indicating or pertaining to one person or thing. *The **singular** form of toys is toy.* **2.** Unusual or peculiar.

skel e ton /skel′ ə tən/ *n.* **1.** The bony framework of the body. *The human **skeleton** is made up of many bones of various shapes and sizes.* **2.** A framework; that to which an outer covering is fastened.

skill /skil/ *n.* Expert ability due to practice or training.

skull /skul/ *n.* The bones that form the framework of the head. *This is the **skull** of a skunk.* [Scandinavian *skul*]

sky scrap er /skī′ skrā′ pər/ *n.* A very tall building. *The invention of the elevator made the **skyscraper** possible.*

smooth /smüŦH/ *adj.* **1.** Not rough. *The lake is **smoother** today than it was yesterday.* **2.** Evenly spread. —*v.* To make even.

smoth er /smuŦH′ ər/ *v.* **1.** To cover, thus keeping out air. *Help me **smother** the fire.* **2.** To kill by depriving something of air. [Old English *smorian,* to suffocate]

so ci e ty /sə sī′ ə tē/ *n., pl.* SOCIETIES. **1.** Companionship or fellowship. *They enjoy one another's **society**.* **2.** Any organization or group joined together for a single purpose. **3.** All people of any given time or place. **4.** The wealthy, fashionable class.

so lu tion /sə lü′ shən/ *n.* **1.** The act or process of solving a problem. *Have you any **solution** for this problem?* **2.** A liquid preparation formed by dissolving a solid, liquid, or gas in a liquid.

som brer o /som brer′ ō/ *n., pl.* SOMBREROS. A wide-brimmed hat, usually of felt or straw, worn especially in Mexico, in Spain, and in the southwestern United States. *Tina bought a **sombrero** as a souvenir of her trip to Mexico.* [Spanish *sombrero*]

spa cious /spā′ shəs/ *adj.* Containing plenty of room; occupying much space.

spa ghet ti /spə get′ ē/ *n.* A type of long, thin noodle. *Spaghetti should not be cooked too long.* [Italian *spaghetti*, little strings]

spec i fy /spes′ ə fī/ *v.*, SPECIFIED, SPECIFYING. To state or name exactly; to mention particularly. *The doctor specified how the drugs should be used.*

spec i men /spes′ ə mən/ *n.* A sample; a portion of anything to show what the rest is like. *Include a specimen of your handwriting along with your application.*

speed boat /spēd′ bōt′/ *n.* A kind of motorboat designed for high speeds.

spell bound /spel′ bound′/ *adj.* Affected as if by a spell; fascinated. *The children sat spellbound throughout the play.*

sphere /sfir/ *n.* **1.** A globe; a ball. *The earth is a sphere flattened at both poles.* **2.** Range or extent, as one's sphere of influence.

splin ter /splin′ tər/ *n.* A sliver; a thin, sharp piece of a material such as wood, bone, or glass. *He removed the splinter from my finger.* —*v.* To split into long, thin pieces.

sponge /spunj/ *n.* An article used for cleaning which is usually soft and highly absorbent. *The sponge quickly absorbed the spilled orange juice.* —*v.*, SPONGED, SPONGING. To wipe up or clean with a sponge. [Latin *spongia*]

spon sor /spon′ sər/ *n.* **1.** A person, organization, or firm which pays for an entertainment, project, or activity. *The sponsor wants the product mentioned on TV.* **2.** A person who takes responsibility for some other person or thing. —*v.* To act as a sponsor.

states man /stāts′ mən/ *n.*, *pl.* STATESMEN. One skilled in public affairs.

stee ple /stē′ pəl/ *n.* A tower that tapers to a point at the top.

straight /strāt/ *adj.* **1.** In a line. *Keep your left margin straight.* **2.** Correct and in order.

straight en /strāt′ ən/ *v.* To make straight. *I can straighten the bent rod.*

strait /strāt/ *n.* A narrow passage of water which connects two larger bodies of water. *The boat passed through the strait.*

strat o sphere /strat′ ə sfir/ *n.* The upper region of the atmosphere. *Clouds seldom form in the stratosphere.*

stretch /strech/ *v.* **1.** To extend or draw out. *See how far this rubber band will stretch.* **2.** To extend one's limbs.

stum ble /stum′ bəl/ *v.*, STUMBLED, STUMBLING. **1.** To trip when walking or running. *He didn't see what made him stumble.* **2.** To walk, talk, or act in an unsteady way.

sub ver sion /səb vėr′ zhən/ *n.* That which undermines or overthrows something or someone. *The FBI guards our country against subversion.*

suc ceed /sək sēd′/ *v.* **1.** To achieve a desired end or result. *The worker succeeded in getting one hundred signatures on the petition.* **2.** To follow or to take the place of another.

suc cess ful /sək ses′ fəl/ *adj.* Having achieved success; prosperous; fortunate.

sul len /sul′ ən/ *adj.* Gloomily silent. *Jack becomes sullen when corrected.*

sum mar y /sum′ ər ē *or* sum′ rē/ *n.*, *pl.* SUMMARIES. A condensed version of a story, a report, etc. *I want you to write a summary of the story.*

sum mit /sum′ it/ *n.* The top. *Did you ever go to the summit of Pikes Peak in Colorado?*

sum mon /sum′ ən/ *v.* **1.** To send for; to call with authority. *The principal summoned the boy to the office.* **2.** To command to appear in court.

sun burn /sun′ bėrn′/ *n.* A burning or inflammation of the skin by the rays of the sun. *Do not expose your skin to bright sun for a long time, or you will get a sunburn.*

---

hat, āge, fär; let, ēqual, tėrm; it, īce; hot, ōpen, ôrder; oil, out; cup, pùt, rüle; ch, child; ng, long; sh, she; th, thin; ᴛʜ, then; zh, measure; ə represents *a* in about, *e* in taken, *i* in pencil, *o* in lemon, *u* in circus.

su per i or /sə pir′ ē ər/ *adj.* **1.** Better; of finer quality. *As a conductor of electricity, copper is* **superior** *to lead.* **2.** Higher in rank or office.

su per vi sion /sü′ pər vizh′ ən/ *n.* Direction and control; oversight. *The* **supervision** *of the employees was Mrs. Smith's job.*

sur geon /sėr′ jən/ *n.* A physician who performs operations.

sur ren der /sə ren′ dər/ *v.* To give up; to yield; to give oneself up. *The enemy* **surrendered** *sooner than we had expected.* — *n.* The act of surrendering.

syn o nym /sin′ ə nim/ *n.* A word that means the same, or almost the same, as another word.

syr up /sir′ əp *or* sėr′ əp/ *n.* A sweet, thick liquid, such as maple syrup.

T

tack le /tak′ əl/ *v.*, TACKLED, TACKLING. To seize with the intent of stopping.

tape re cord er /tāp′ ri kôr′ dər/ *n.* An instrument that records music, speech, etc., on tape. *Wait until you see the* **tape recorder** *my mom bought me for my birthday.*

tech ni cal /tek′ nə kəl/ *adj.* **1.** Pertaining to mechanical skills and science. *Since I want to be an electrician, I plan to go to a* **technical** *school.* **2.** Peculiar to a particular trade or profession.

te di ous /tē′ dē əs *or* tē′ jəs/ *adj.* Slow, dull, and tiresome. *Won't you help me with this* **tedious** *work?*

ten sion /ten′ shən/ *n.* **1.** A stretching or a stretched condition. *The* **tension** *of the strings determines the tone of a guitar.* **2.** Mental or emotional strain.

the or y /thē′ ər ē *or* thir′ ē/ *n., pl.* THEORIES. **1.** A reasonable explanation of a problem. *Columbus proved the* **theory** *that the earth*

is round. **2.** General or basic principles of a science or an art.

thirst /thėrst/ *n.* **1.** A craving for something. *The young actor had a* **thirst** *for fame.* **2.** The sensation caused by a desire or need for water. — *v.* **1.** To crave or desire something. **2.** To have a strong desire or need for water. [Old English *thurst*]

this tle /this′ əl/ *n.* A plant which has prickly leaves and stems.

thrift /thrift/ *n.* Wise management of money; saving. *Do you know the value of* **thrift?** [Scandinavian *thrif*]

tis sue /tish′ ü/ *n.* **1.** A group of similar cells in a plant or animal that works together to perform a particular function. *To mend the torn* **tissue,** *the doctor wrapped my ankle with an elastic bandage.* **2.** A cloth of thin, lightweight material. **3.** A kind of thin, soft paper that absorbs moisture easily.

tol e rate /tol′ ə rāt′/ *v.*, TOLERATED, TOLERATING. **1.** To endure. *I may* **tolerate** *the condition, but I do not encourage it.* **2.** To allow by not hindering.

touch down /tuch′ doun′/ *n.* The score made in football by the placing of the ball behind the opponent's goal lines. *The visiting team made the first* **touchdown.**

trac tion /trak′ shən/ *n.* Friction. *When there is too little* **traction,** *the wheels of a car will slip.*

trans con ti nen tal /trans′ kon tə nen′ təl/ *adj.* Passing across a continent.

tran scribe /tran skrib′/ *v.*, TRANSCRIBED, TRANSCRIBING. **1.** To reproduce material previously prepared, as on radio or television. *The network will* **transcribe** *Mr. Smith's speech this evening.* **2.** To make a copy of something. **3.** To write or type from shorthand notes.

trans fu sion /tran sfyü′ zhən/ *n.* The transferring of blood from one person or animal to another.

trans pose /trans pōz´/ *v.*, TRANSPOSED, TRANSPOSING. To interchange. *You will have to* **transpose** *the i and the e in that word if you want to spell it correctly.*

trea son /trē´ zən/ *n.* The act or crime of betraying one's own government or state. *It would be* **treason** *to help the enemy in time of war.*

treas ur y /trezh´ ər ē *or* trezh´ rē/ *n., pl.* TREASURIES. 1. A place where money or other valuables are kept. *Last summer we saw the* **Treasury** *of the United States.* 2. The financial department of an organization. 3. The funds belonging to a particular organization.

tre men dous /tri men´ dəs/ *adj.* 1. Extremely large or great. *The explosion was* **tremendous.** 2. Extraordinary.

trop i cal /trop´ ə kəl/ *adj.* 1. Pertaining to the tropics. *There are many* **tropical** *birds in the Everglades of Florida.* 2. Hot and humid.

trus tee /tru stē´/ *n., pl.* TRUSTEES. One responsible for the property or business affairs of another or of an institution. *Mr. Edwards is a* **trustee** *of the museum.* [Scandinavian *traust,* trust]

turn pike /tèrn´ pīk´/ *n.* A toll road. *The new* **turnpike** *will avoid large cities.*

typ i cal /tip´ ə kəl/ *adj.* Like others of the same kind; representative.

U

un der mine /un´ dər mīn´ *or* un´ dər mīn´/ *v.*, UNDERMINED, UNDERMINING. To weaken or ruin by degrees; to hinder. *In time, lack of sleep can help to* **undermine** *one's health.*

u nique /yü nēk´/ *adj.* 1. Different from anything else. *Each speaker made a* **unique** *contribution to the discussion.* 2. Unequaled.

us a ble /yü´ zə bəl/ *adj.* Suitable for use. *Don't throw those nails away; they are still* **usable.**

use ful /yüs´ fəl/ *adj.* Serviceable; practical. *A coffeepot is a* **useful** *gift.*

V

val iant /val´ yənt/ *adj.* Brave; courageous. *The two helicopter pilots were praised for their* **valiant** *rescue of the mountain climbers.*

va moose /va müs´ *or* və müs´/ *v.*, VAMOOSED, VAMOOSING. *Slang.* To leave quickly. *The angry farmer ordered the hunters to* **vamoose.** [Spanish *vamos*]

va nil la /və nil´ ə/ *n.* A flavoring extract made from the seed of a plant. *Vanilla is my favorite flavoring.* —*adj.* Having the flavor of or derived from vanilla.

van ish /van´ ish/ *v.* To disappear. *The deer* **vanished** *as suddenly as it had appeared.* [French *evanir*]

va por /vā´ pər/ *n.* 1. Mist or other moisture visible in the air. *Vapor rose from the spout of the teakettle.* 2. The gas formed from a substance that ordinarily is a solid or liquid.

var nish /vär´ nish/ *n.* A liquid substance which leaves a smooth, glossy appearance when it is applied to wood, metal, etc. *I gave the wood floor an extra coat of* **varnish.** —*v.* To apply varnish.

vi cious /vish´ əs/ *adj.* 1. Evil or wicked. *A series of* **vicious** *crimes caused panic throughout the neighborhood.* 2. Fierce; savage. 3. Spiteful; bitter.

vic tim /vik´ təm/ *n.* An animal or a person injured or destroyed as a result of accident, disease, or other misfortune. *The dog was the* **victim** *of the master's bad temper.*

vic to ri ous /vik tôr´ ē əs *or* vik tōr´ ē əs/ *adj.*

---

hat, āge, fär; let, ēqual, tèrm; it, īce; hot, ōpen, ôrder; oil, out; cup, pút, rüle; ch, child; ng, long; sh, she; th, thin; ᴛʜ, then; zh, measure; ə represents *a* in about, *e* in taken, *i* in pencil, *o* in lemon, *u* in circus.

Having achieved a victory; triumphant. *The **victorious** team was honored at a special banquet.*

vic tor y /vik′ tər ē *or* vik′ trē/ *n., pl.* VICTOR- IES. The defeat of an enemy or rival. *Our third baseball game was our first **victory** of the season.*

vil lain /vil′ ən/ *n.* A scoundrel; one guilty or capable of a crime. *I was pleased when the **villain** in the play was punished.*

vin e gar /vin′ ə gər/ *n.* A sour liquid, often made from cider or wine, used for flavoring or for preserving something. *The cucumbers were pickled in **vinegar**.*

vir tu ous /vėr′ chü əs *or* vėrch′ wəs/ *adj.* Good; moral; pure. *A **virtuous** person always tries to do what is best.*

vis i ble /viz′ ə bəl/ *adj.* Capable of being seen. *Some stars are so far away that they are not **visible** to the naked eye.*

vis u al /vizh′ ü əl *or* vizh′ wəl/ *adj.* Having to do with vision or sight. *Motion pictures are a popular **visual** aid used in many class- rooms.*

vis u al ize /vizh′ ü ə līz *or* vizh′ wə līz′/ *v.,* VISUALIZED, VISUALIZING. To picture in the mind. *Can you **visualize** what a new dam will do for this valley?*

vi ta min /vī′ tə min/ *n.* Any one of a number of elements found in foods in their natural state that are essential for the proper nour- ishment of people and animals. *Citrus fruits are rich in **vitamins**.*

vol ca no /vol kā′ nō/ *n., pl.* VOLCANOS OR VOLCANOES. A mountain or hill having a crater from which steam, lava, hot rocks, and gases pour forth. *Are there any active volcanos in the United States?* [Latin *Vul- canus*, god of fire]

W

weird /wird/ *adj.* Uncanny; unearthly; strange. *We heard a **weird** sound as we walked through the woods.*

wheth er /hweŦH′ ər/ *conj.* A word of doubt used to introduce a choice or to indicate several possibilities. *I don't know **whether** I'll go or not.*

wield /wēld/ *v.* To handle or use with skill; to employ. *That artist **wielded** his brush to great advantage.*

wie ner /wē′ nər/ *n.* A small sausage; a frank- furter. *We roasted **wieners** over the campfire we had built.*

wind shield /wind′ shēld′/ *n.* A shield of glass to protect the occupants of a car from rain, wind, etc. *The driver brushed the snow off the **windshield** before attempting to drive.*

wrench /rench/ *v.* To injure by twisting or pull- ing. *In lifting that box, be careful not to **wrench** your back.* —*n.* **1.** A violent twisting. **2.** An instrument for turning or loosening bolts.

Y

yield /yēld/ *v.* **1.** To give up; to surrender. *The car on the left must **yield** the right of way.* **2.** To bring forth, as to yield a crop. —*n.* The amount produced.

yolk /yōk/ *n.* The yellow part of an egg. *Try not to break the **yolk** when you fry the egg.*